Principles of Banking and Insurance

Prof. C. Arun Kumar

Dr. C. Revathy

Principles of Banking and Insurance

Prof. C. Arun Kumar
SRMIST, FSH, Vadapalani Campus

Dr. C. Revathy
Guru Nanak College, Chennai

This book is dedicated to our students, expressing heartfelt gratitude and love.

- AK & CR

About the Book

In today's rapidly changing economic environment and shifting financial landscape, studying banking and insurance is essential for comprehending the complex mechanisms that underpin our financial systems. This comprehensive textbook is thoughtfully designed for finance students and enthusiasts, guiding readers through the multifaceted domains of banking and insurance.

The first section of the book explores the foundational aspects of banking, including the processes of credit creation, reserve requirements, and the regulatory structures that govern financial institutions. It examines the role of the Reserve Bank of India (RBI), alongside public, private, and foreign banks, offering an extensive overview of the banking sector's evolution, from the nationalization of banks to the establishment of institutions like NABARD and regional rural banks.

Further, the book delves into lending practices, covering topics such as priority sector lending, base and prime lending rates, and the critical role of deposit mobilization. It also addresses challenges like non-performing assets (NPAs) and provides insight into remedies that promote the banking sector's stability and resilience.

The book then discusses major regulatory changes, including the Narasimhan Committee recommendations, interest rate deregulation, and the adoption of capital adequacy and BASEL norms.

In the second section, the focus shifts to insurance, covering fundamental concepts, definitions, and the economic and legal principles of risk pooling and transfer. This section examines the distinctions between social and private insurance, as well as categories within life, health, and general insurance.

Finally, the textbook explores advanced concepts in risk management, including expected utility, moral hazard, and the demand for insurance. The chapter provides a global perspective on reinsurance, examining essential aspects such as risk assessment, control, and financing.

With sincere dedication, we offer this textbook to students, aspiring to deepen their understanding of banking and insurance. We hope it serves as a valuable resource in shaping knowledgeable and skilled professionals within the finance sector.

About the Author(s)

Prof. C. Arun Kumar is an experienced Assistant Professor in Commerce, currently serving at SRM IST, Chennai in the Department of Commerce (Honors – International Accounting and Finance). He holds part-time and visiting faculty positions at the University of Madras, LIBA, and Loyola-PULC, with previous roles including Assistant Professor & Head (CS) at Don Bosco Arts & Science College and visiting faculty at Indian Maritime University and Ramakrishna Vivekananda College.

Prof. Arun Kumar has published 7 research articles in UGC-Care listed journals, presented at 5 national and 2 international conferences, and serves as a special lecturer for UGC-NET at USAB, University of Madras.

Over the past 4 years, he has organized 11 national seminars and 2 international conferences. Certified as a career coach, Prof. Arun Kumar has guided over 500 students and authored 2 books. He mentors research scholars and students in statistical tools like SPSS and Advanced Excel and has delivered over 50 special lectures on career development, financial, and management topics. His YouTube channel, "Prof. C. Arun Kumar," boasts over 33,000 subscribers.

Dr. C. Revathy is an Assistant Professor in the PG & Research Department of Commerce, Guru Nanak College, Chennai. She has more than 16 years of teaching experience, and her areas of expertise are marketing, financial management, and accounting.

She is a university-recognized supervisor who is currently guiding 4 scholars and a project guide at IGNOU. She was an organizing committee member in two national, two international conference, member of editorial board and organized multiple workshop and entrepreneurial programs. For her great teaching, she has won various honors and accolades, including the "Best faculty award 2022" at GMRAF in Chennai and the "Best outstanding academical national award 2020" at Kamarjar Institute in Theni.

She has participated in numerous FDPs and conferences, and has published over 23 research papers. She has served as a career and professional skill mentor for commerce students and as a resource person in numerous seminars.

Preface

In the intricate tapestry of modern economies, the roles played by banking and insurance are integral threads that weave together financial stability, risk management, and economic progress. The textbook endeavors to shed light on the profound significance of these two domains, offering readers a nuanced understanding of their roles, functions, and the broader impact they exert on societies and individuals.

Banking, as the financial backbone of economies, facilitates the flow of capital, fosters economic growth, and supports businesses and individuals in their financial endeavors. From the creation of credit to the regulatory frameworks that ensure stability, the banking sector is a cornerstone of economic vitality. This book aims to demystify the complexities of banking, providing a holistic view of its evolution, regulatory landscape, and its social responsibilities.

Simultaneously, the world of insurance stands as a crucial mechanism for mitigating and managing risk. Insurance, whether in life, health, or general forms, acts as a safeguard against uncertainties, offering individuals and businesses the resilience to navigate unforeseen challenges. Through an exploration of foundational principles, economic perspectives, and global considerations, this textbook seeks to illuminate the pivotal role insurance plays in promoting financial security and societal well-being.

As we embark on this exploration, we invite readers to delve into the intricacies of banking and insurance with an open mind and a keen interest. The pages that follow aim not only to impart knowledge but also to cultivate a deep appreciation for the critical functions these sectors perform in sustaining the economic fabric of our interconnected world.

May this textbook serve as a gateway for students, professionals, and enthusiasts to grasp the essence of banking and insurance, inspiring a commitment to the responsible stewardship of financial systems and the promotion of economic well-being.

Brief Contents

Unit 1: Banks – definition-process of credit creation – reserve requirements – banking regulation act – role of RBI – type of banks – PSU banks – private and foreign banks –NABARD and rural banks – nationalization of banks – expansion of branches and social role of banks.

Unit 2: Priority sector lending – other lending – base rate and prime lending rate – deposit mobilization – composition of deposits and lending – consortium of banks – NPA – issues and remedies.

Unit 3: Narasimham committee of banking reforms – changes in banking regulation – deregulation of interest rates – capital adequacy and BASEL norms – governance issues.

Unit 4: Insurance – basic issues – definition of insurance – risk pooling and risk transfer – economic and legal perspectives, social vs private insurance – life vs non-life insurance – classification of life, health and general insurance policies.

Unit 5: Expected utility and demand for insurance – moral hazard and insurance demand – concept of risk management – essentials of risk management – elements of risk management – risk assessment – risk control and risk financing – worldwide risk sharing – concept of reinsurance – fundamentals of reinsurance – types of reinsurers – reinsurance distribution systems – reinsurance markets in developing countries

Table of Content

UNIT I FUNDAMENTALS OF BANKING

Chapter 1 Introduction to Banking

According to the **Collins Reference Dictionary of Economics (1988)**, a bank is defined as an institution legally authorized to accept public deposits, holding funds for safekeeping with the obligation to repay depositors upon request, such as through a cheque. In contemporary terms, the American Institute of Banking describes a bank as an intermediary that facilitates transactions between lenders and borrowers, making it central to a complex financial structure.

Banking forms the backbone of modern economies, acting as a pivotal element in facilitating financial transactions, promoting economic growth, and ensuring the efficient flow of funds. This introductory chapter sets the stage by examining the fundamental concepts and key roles that banks play within the financial sector.

At its essence, banking covers a broad range of activities, from the basic function of safeguarding funds to more advanced roles in credit creation and risk management. By connecting savers with those in need of capital, banks direct funds into productive areas of the economy, contributing to financial system stability and broader economic development.

1.1. The Credit Creation Process:

A unique feature of banking is its capacity for credit creation. By providing loans, mortgages, and other financial services, banks can expand the money supply, which in turn stimulates economic activity. Grasping the mechanics of credit creation is key to understanding the broader influence banks exert on economic growth and development.

Regulatory Framework and the Banking Regulation Act:

The banking industry functions within a structured regulatory framework designed to uphold stability, integrity, and ethical practices. The Banking Regulation Act serves as the legal cornerstone for bank governance, defining allowable activities, capital standards, and oversight mechanisms.

The Role of the Reserve Bank of India (RBI):

In India, the Reserve Bank of India (RBI) serves as the central banking authority with a critical role in maintaining economic stability. Along with regulating and overseeing banks, the RBI shapes monetary policy, issues currency, and functions as the lender of last resort, making substantial contributions to the nation's economic resilience.

Diversity in Types of Banks:

The banking sector is made up of a range of institutions, each serving different needs and customer groups. Public Sector Undertaking (PSU) banks, private banks, and foreign banks all play unique roles and contribute differently to the financial ecosystem. Recognizing these distinctions is key to understanding the diversity and dynamism within the banking industry.

NABARD, Rural Banks, and Nationalization:

The National Bank for Agriculture and Rural Development (NABARD) and rural banks are vital parts of the banking system, tailored to meet the financial requirements of rural communities. The nationalization of banks was a landmark decision aimed at broadening access to financial services and fostering economic inclusivity.

1.2.Expansion and Social Role of Banks:

The expansion of bank branches and their social roles go beyond mere financial transactions. Banks serve as catalysts for community development, financial education, and empowerment. Examining their broader societal impact provides insights into the multifaceted nature of banking.

The objectives of a bank differ from those of other financial institutions, with a broader perspective often seen as more influential within the financial industry. Three distinct viewpoints can be considered when analyzing a bank's goals:

- The objective from the perspective of bank owners
- The purpose from the government's viewpoint
- The goal from the perspective of bank clients

The aim from the perspective of bank owners

- **Making a profit:** Like any other business, the bank's owners are motivated by the desire to make money. This is why they engage in the banking industry.

- **Providing Services**: As part of their social responsibility, banks offer a variety of services to society, making this a key objective. Banks are not just focused on profit but also on contributing positively to the community.

- **Investment of Funds**: Bank owners view the bank as an ideal avenue to invest their accumulated savings, helping to grow their wealth.

- **Earning Goodwill**: Bank owners see the institution as a means of building goodwill, expanding the reach of their banking operations and enhancing their reputation.

- **Raising Efficiency**: By ensuring the smooth functioning of their banking operations, bank owners work to sharpen their managerial skills and improve overall efficiency.

The purpose from the perspective of the government

- **Issuance of Notes and Currency**: The government issues currency notes through banks, which serve as a medium of exchange in the economy.
- **Capital Formation**: The government actively encourages capital formation within society, with banks playing a pivotal role as catalysts in fostering capital creation across various sectors.
- **Capital investment and industrialization:** The bank promotes industrialization by assisting with appropriate capital investments through its numerous asset offerings. In the long run, this promotes GDP expansion, reduces poverty, and ensures wealth distribution on an equal basis.
- **Money market control:** A bank's varied products help to regulate the availability of money on the market and keep the economy from overheating.
- **Creation of employment opportunities:** The bank will create a lot of jobs to meet its demand for human resources.
- **Financial counselling:** Banks occasionally make good ideas to the government regarding finances.

The goal from the perspective of bank customers

- **Safe Custodian of Public Funds:** Banks act as secure custodians for public money, providing peace of mind to depositors by protecting their funds from theft, robbery, or loss.
- **Custodian of Public Funds**: In addition to safeguarding funds, banks often serve as financial advisors, guiding clients on various financial matters.

- **Representative or Trustee:** At times, banks take on the role of a representative or trustee, managing assets or acting on behalf of their clients.
- **Offering Credit Facilities:** Banks provide loan services, offering customers the opportunity to invest in profitable ventures and generate returns.

Chapter 2 The Process of Credit Creation

A bank's unique ability to create credit distinguishes it from other financial institutions. Credit creation refers to the expansion of deposits. Banks can multiply their cash reserves through demand deposits, which are the primary means of exchange.

The key component of the money supply is "demand deposits." As these deposits grow, the overall money circulating in the economy increases. Credit forms the backbone of the banking system, defined as obtaining purchasing power today with the promise of repayment in the future.

Bank credit includes both advances and loans. Banks maintain only a small fraction of reserves to meet withdrawal demands, using the rest to issue loans and generate profit. When a loan is made, the amount is credited to the borrower's account, and a corresponding deposit is created in the lending bank. Consequently, an increase in bank deposits leads to the creation of more credit.

2.1. The Two Crucial Elements of Credit

a) **Liquidity Creation:** When banks utilize their legal power to demand cash from their depositors, they are required to pay cash to their depositors.

b) **Profit Making:** Banks, as profit-driven businesses, constantly aim to maximize earnings. This is why they must make strategic loan decisions that yield higher interest returns than the interest paid on their deposits.

A bank's credit policy is founded on the assumption that only a small fraction of its clients will need to withdraw cash at any given time. Conversely, banks operate under the expectation that not all clients will demand cash simultaneously from their accounts.

Understand the Fundamental Principles of Credit Creation

a) Bank as a Business Entity: Banks should be viewed as commercial entities that continually strive to boost profits through loans and advances secured by deposits.

b) Bank Deposits: Credit is generated based on the foundation of bank deposits.

The two forms of bank deposits are as follows:

- **Primary Deposits:** When a bank receives cash from clients and creates a deposit in the client's name, it is referred to as a primary deposit. This is not considered credit creation. Essentially, these deposits convert currency money into deposit money, forming the base for credit generation.
- **Secondary or Derivative Deposits:** When a bank provides loans or advances, it does not disburse cash directly. Instead, it creates a deposit account in the borrower's name. This type of deposit is known as a secondary or derivative deposit.

Every loan creates a deposit and the creation of a derivative deposit means the creation of the credit.

2.2. Credit Creation Process by Commercial Banks

The central bank is the primary source of a country's money supply through the circulation of currency. It ensures there is enough money available to meet the transaction needs of the economy. By doing so, it facilitates various economic processes such as production, distribution, and consumption. To achieve this, the central bank depends on commercial bank reserves, which serve as the secondary source of the money supply in the economy.

The issuance of credit is a commercial bank's primary goal. This explains why the currency provided by commercial banks is referred to as credit money. By making loans and buying securities, commercial banks all contribute to the creation of credit. They use public deposits received as deposits to make loans to both individuals and corporations.

Commercial banks cannot use the entire amount of public deposits for lending. They are required to maintain a certain portion as reserves with the central bank to ensure they can meet depositors' withdrawal needs. Once the required reserve is set aside, the remaining public deposits can be lent out by the commercial banks.

Factors Affecting Commercial Banks' Ability to Create Credit

The following are some factors that affect how credit is created:

- **Bank's Credit Creation Power:** A bank's ability to create credit is directly linked to the amount of cash deposited with it. The ratio of cash reserves to deposits also influences the bank's capacity to generate credit.
- **Need for Credit Generation:** Banks must generate credit to support economic activity and their business operations.
- **Market Demand for Credit:** The level of credit creation is also influenced by the market's demand for credit.

2.3. Benefits and Drawbacks of Commercial Banks' Credit Creation

Positive Aspects:

Depositors benefit from easy access to a wide range of products offered by intermediaries, many of which can be quickly converted into cash. Additionally, shares in companies (such as mutual funds) can be easily sold when needed.

Negative Aspects:

Access to Diverse Products: Commercial banks offer a variety of financial products and services, including savings accounts, fixed deposits, loans, and credit cards. This diverse selection allows depositors to choose options that best meet their financial goals.

Liquidity and Quick Conversion: Products offered by intermediaries are highly liquid, meaning they can be rapidly converted into cash. This liquidity provides depositors with quick access to funds, offering financial flexibility.

Investment Opportunities: Commercial banks facilitate investment opportunities for depositors by offering services such as mutual funds. Depositors can invest in shares of companies through these funds, providing a convenient way to participate in the financial markets.

Efficient Disposal of Investments: Investments made through mutual funds or other financial instruments can be quickly and efficiently disposed of, allowing depositors to manage their portfolios and respond to changing financial conditions.

Drawbacks of Commercial Banks' Credit Creation:

Lack of Security: There is a risk associated with investments, and depositors may face losses if the market experiences downturns. Unlike traditional savings accounts, certain investment products do not guarantee the safety of principal.

Commercial Environment Risks: The financial stability of commercial banks is closely tied to the broader economic climate. Economic recessions or adverse market conditions can negatively impact the performance of banks, thereby affecting the returns on their investments.

Lack of Funds: Credit creation by commercial banks relies on the availability of funds, and limitations in funds may constrain the ability to extend credit. This can impact the overall economic activities and growth potential of businesses.

People's Customs and Behavioral Factors: Customer behavior, financial literacy, and adherence to financial customs can influence the effectiveness of credit creation. Mismanagement of funds, defaults on loans, or lack of understanding of financial products can lead to adverse consequences.

Leakages in the System: The credit creation process may have leakages where not all funds injected into the system contribute to economic growth. Some funds may be used for speculative purposes or diverted away from productive activities, leading to inefficiencies.

Chapter 3 Reserve Requirements

3.1. Reserve Requirements in the Indian Banking System

The Reserve Bank of India (RBI) determines and regulates reserve requirements in India's banking system. However, given the evolving nature of regulatory and monetary frameworks, it's crucial to stay updated with the latest RBI guidelines. The RBI's Monetary Policy Committee, which conducts regular meetings at least four times a year, adjusts monetary policy and issues related guidelines.

Statutory Liquidity Ratio (SLR)

The SLR is a mandatory reserve requirement compelling commercial banks in India to maintain a minimum percentage of their Net Demand and Time Liabilities (NDTL) in liquid assets like cash, gold, or government-approved securities. Its purpose is to ensure banks' liquidity and solvency and to control credit expansion. Traditionally, SLR has been set between 18-20% of NDTL, with the current rate at 18% (as of December 14, 2023). The RBI has established a cap, allowing SLR to go up to a maximum of 40%.

Cash Reserve Ratio (CRR)

CRR is another form of reserve requirement governed by the RBI, mandating banks to maintain a certain portion of their deposits in cash with the central bank. The primary purpose of CRR is to stabilize the money supply within the economy. Generally, CRR rates are lower than SLR and fluctuate according to economic conditions. The CRR has historically varied based on RBI's approach to liquidity management. As of December 14, 2023, the CRR rate stands at 4%.

Changes and Adjustments

The RBI holds the authority to modify these reserve requirements as part of its monetary policy toolkit. Adjustments to SLR and CRR are based on economic assessments, inflation rates, financial liquidity, and other economic factors.

Impact on Banking Operations

Compliance with reserve requirements directly influences banks' lending and investment capacities. Through SLR and CRR adjustments, the RBI aims to control the money supply, affect interest rates, and curb inflation.

Periodic Reviews

The RBI regularly reviews and, if necessary, modifies reserve requirements. These adjustments are typically announced beforehand, giving banks adequate time to adjust their portfolios.

The Concept of Cash Reserve Ratios

Cash reserve requirements, commonly referred to as reserve ratios, denote the portion of deposits banks are mandated to keep in reserve. This measure ensures banks can handle sudden spikes in withdrawals and is an essential aspect of central banking policy. In India, banks may reserve deposits in the RBI or as cash within their own safes. These requirements provide a tool for the central bank (RBI) to control the monetary flow, thus influencing interest rates and overall economic stability.

3.2. How Reserve Requirements Work

Banks are required to hold a portion of their deposits as reserves, either in cash or with the central bank. This arrangement allows banks to lend the remaining portion of deposits, generating interest income. If banks hold excessive reserves, they may miss opportunities to earn returns through lending. Conversely, if they hold insufficient reserves, they risk insolvency and potential issues during a bank run. Laws require commercial banks to comply with reserve requirements, with the RBI responsible for calculating and reviewing these needs.

Significance of Reserve Requirements

Reserve requirements equip banks to face future obligations, serving as a buffer against unexpected economic shocks. By regulating reserve levels, the central bank can indirectly manage loan issuance, deposit rates, and liquidity in the market. For example, if State Bank of India (SBI) experiences an unexpected downturn, it can use its reserves to address impending liabilities.

3.3. Reasons for Reserve Requirements

Reserve requirements serve multiple purposes, primarily to control the flow of money in the economy. Through these requirements, the RBI regulates the growth in money supply and liquidity within the money market. A high reserve ratio can reduce market liquidity. Reserve requirements also safeguard public deposits, ensuring that banks are adequately prepared to handle unforeseen scenarios.

Example of Reserve Requirement Calculation

Consider that SBI receives a Rs. 3,000 demand deposit and Rs. 50-time deposit, with an 8% reserve requirement ratio. The total reserve requirement calculation would be:

- **Demand Deposits**: 8% of Rs. 3,000 = Rs. 240
- **Time Deposits**: 0% of Rs. 50 = Rs. 0
- **Total Reserve Requirement** = Rs. 240

3.4. Capital Requirements vs. Reserve Requirements

Reserve requirements ensure banks have the liquidity to address liabilities or unexpected increases in withdrawals. Capital requirements, on the other hand, ensure banks maintain sufficient capital to cover the loans or other credit services they provide. While reserve requirements manage liquidity and safeguard against withdrawal risks, capital requirements act as a buffer for loan or credit losses.

Advantages of Reserve Requirements

- **Uniform Impact on Banks**: All banks must comply with the reserve requirements equally, significantly affecting money availability in the economy.
- **Economic Liquidity Assurance**: It ensures that the economy has sufficient liquidity to handle economic fluctuations.
- **Maximization of Loan Potential**: By regulating reserves, banks can take advantage of lending opportunities, thereby maximizing profitability.

- **Risk Management**: Reserve requirements equip banks to address unforeseen events such as cash shortages, sudden withdrawals, or excessive lending.
- **Depositor Awareness**: Reserve requirements enhance depositor trust by ensuring banks are financially sound.

Disadvantages of Reserve Requirements

- **Unrealistic Expectations**: Adjusting cash-reserve ratios even slightly can drastically affect money availability, leading to increased costs for banks.
- **Liquidity Constraints**: For banks with low excess reserves, meeting reserve requirements can result in liquidity issues.

In summary, reserve requirements function as a regulatory measure, compelling banks to retain a portion of deposits as a buffer against unexpected withdrawals. While referred to as "cash reserves," the approach has limitations in terms of practicality but remains an essential component of banking stability.

Chapter 4 Banking Regulation Act

The **Banking Regulation Act, 1949**, also known initially as the Banking Companies Act of 1949, serves as the foundational legal framework that regulates all banking institutions in India. Enacted on **March 16, 1949**, it was renamed on **March 1, 1966** to expand its scope. Since **1956**, it has applied to Jammu and Kashmir as well. Originally focusing only on banking companies, the Act underwent several modifications to incorporate cooperative banks (in **1965** under Section 56) and to establish regulations governing their operations, while giving the **Reserve Bank of India (RBI)** regulatory authority. The Act now addresses both commercial and cooperative banks, ensuring a robust, supervised banking ecosystem across India.

Scope and Powers of the Banking Regulation Act

The Act grants the RBI comprehensive powers, such as:

- **Granting Licenses** to banks, determining their eligibility to operate.
- **Regulating Shareholding and Voting Rights** of shareholders, to prevent undue influence in banking operations.
- **Supervising Board Composition** of banks, ensuring that skilled and qualified individuals govern banking institutions.
- **Managing Bank Operations** by establishing guidelines, monitoring policies, and penalizing non-compliance.
- **Setting Operational Standards** for bank inspections, audits, mergers, acquisitions, and public welfare mandates.
- **Penalizing Violations** to maintain the stability of the banking sector.

The **Banking Regulation (Amendment) Bill, 2020**, was introduced by Finance Minister Nirmala Sitharaman, bringing new modifications to improve operational guidelines, with significant emphasis on cooperative banks. This amendment allows for cooperative banks to be under stricter RBI oversight, safeguarding depositors' interests and enhancing banking stability.

4.1 Key Provisions of the Banking Regulation Act, 1949

Some of the significant sections of the Act include:

- **Prohibition on Trading Activities (Section 8)**: Prohibits banks from engaging in direct or indirect product trading. Banks can, however, handle transactions related to trade bills or currency exchange.
- **Restriction on Holding Non-banking Assets (Section 9)**: Banks cannot retain immovable properties (non-banking assets) indefinitely. Properties acquired must be sold within seven years unless RBI grants an extension.
- **Management Standards (Section 10)**: This section mandates that bank boards be led by knowledgeable individuals in fields such as finance, agriculture, and law. At least 51% of the board members must possess expertise in relevant areas.
- **Minimum Capital Requirements (Section 11(2))**: Banks must maintain minimum paid-up capital as approved by the RBI before they can commence or continue operations.
- **Commission Payment Restriction (Section 13)**: Prohibits banks from paying commissions or fees exceeding 2.5% of the nominal value of their shares for transactions, to prevent overcompensation.

- **Dividend Payout Restriction (Section 15)**: Banks are barred from paying dividends unless initial capital expenses, association costs, and all outstanding expenses have been fully addressed.

4.2. Latest Features and Regulations under the Act

The Act has adapted to the evolving financial landscape with key regulatory features that include:

- **Centralized Supervision by the RBI**: Empowers the RBI to supervise all commercial banks to ensure compliance, stability, and operational transparency.
- **Licensing and Operational Control**: The RBI issues licenses to banks, conducts routine inspections, and enforces compliance with financial standards.
- **Capital Adequacy Requirement**: Sets a minimum capital threshold to secure banks' solvency against unexpected losses, maintaining a stable financial system.
- **Restrictions on Dividends and Lending**: Limits banks' dividend payouts, ensuring profits are prudently reinvested, while setting lending limits to directors and related parties to avoid conflicts of interest.
- **Transparency and Disclosure Mandates**: Requires banks to disclose information such as fees and interest rates, fostering an environment of transparency for customers.
- **Grievance Redressal Mechanisms**: Provides avenues for customers to seek redressal, promoting fair banking practices and accountability.
- **Prohibition of Unfair Trade Practices**: Prevents banks from misleading customers through false advertising or concealed fees, ensuring ethical banking practices.

- **Restrictions on Non-banking Activities**: Prohibits banks from engaging in non-core activities like real estate or commodity trading, to reduce financial risks and focus on banking operations.
- **Data Privacy and Security**: Sets standards for safeguarding customer information, regulating data handling to protect against unauthorized access.

4.3 Importance of the Banking Regulation Act, 1949

The Banking Regulation Act is a crucial component of the Indian financial regulatory framework. Here are the key reasons behind its significance:

- **Empowers the RBI as a Regulatory Authority**: The Act strengthens the RBI's capacity to oversee and guide the Indian banking sector, ensuring its stability.
- **Framework for Licensing**: Defines the criteria for establishing banks in India, ensuring only entities that meet specific standards are allowed to operate.
- **Capital Adequacy and Stability**: Requires banks to hold adequate capital to cover potential losses, thereby enhancing the stability of both individual banks and the broader financial system.
- **Governance and Operational Standards**: Sets guidelines for the composition and management of banks, ensuring a professionally managed and ethical approach to banking operations.
- **Customer Protection**: Protects depositors' interests by mandating transparency, accountability, and ethical practices in banking.
- **Prevention of Monopoly and Concentration of Power**: Limits the accumulation of economic power within a few

entities by regulating ownership, ensuring a competitive banking environment.

- **Regulates Bank Activities**: Specifies permitted and prohibited activities for banks, ensuring they focus on core banking services and avoid unnecessary risks.
- **Resolution Mechanisms for Banking Failures**: Outlines the procedure for handling distressed banks, giving RBI authority to take corrective measures or intervene.
- **Amendments to Address Evolving Challenges**: Adapts to the changing financial sector through amendments, keeping the regulatory framework relevant and effective.
- **Global Compliance and Best Practices**: Aligns the Indian banking system with international regulatory standards, boosting confidence in Indian banks on a global scale.

The **Banking Regulation Act, 1949** is a vital regulatory law that lays down the framework for the direction and control of the banking sector in India. Encompassing a range of areas from governance to customer protection and regulatory oversight, it plays a central role in maintaining a stable and efficient banking system. The RBI's regulatory authority, as established by this Act, has been instrumental in creating a financially robust and transparent banking environment that aligns with international standards. Furthermore, its adaptability over the years, with significant amendments like those in 1965 for cooperative banks and 2020 for enhanced supervision, reflects its responsiveness to the changing dynamics of the banking sector.

Chapter 5 Role of Reserve Bank of India

The Reserve Bank of India (RBI) plays a pivotal role in the Indian economy, offering a range of services to maintain financial stability and promote growth. Headquartered in Mumbai, the RBI was established in 1935 under the Reserve Bank of India Act of 1934, influenced by the recommendations of the Hilton-Young Commission in 1926. Initially founded as a privately-owned institution, it was nationalized in 1949 to align the central bank's policies with the government's economic goals, reflecting the priorities of a newly independent India.

The RBI's objectives are clearly stated in its preamble:

- To control the issuance of banknotes.
- To maintain monetary stability in India.
- To manage the currency and credit system for India's advantage.

Through comprehensive supervision, the RBI regulates commercial banks, non-banking financial companies (NBFCs), and financial institutions to uphold public confidence and ensure a sound banking system. Over time, it has adapted to the evolving economy, making significant adjustments to its functions and responsibilities.

5.1. Key Functions of RBI

- **Monetary Authority**: The RBI formulates and implements monetary policy to stabilize prices and foster growth. By balancing inflation control with growth objectives, it ensures economic stability, adapting measures to meet changing economic conditions.

- **Supervisor and Regulator of the Financial System**: As a regulator, the RBI sets guidelines for India's banking and financial systems, ensuring public trust. Its regulatory framework aims to protect depositors' interests and provide affordable banking services to the public.

- **Manager of Foreign Exchange**: The RBI administers the Foreign Exchange Management Act (FEMA), 1999, to encourage foreign trade, manage external payments, and promote a stable foreign exchange market. This role includes safeguarding the rupee's value and supporting India's trade and investment flows.

- **Issuer of Currency**: The RBI is the sole issuer of currency notes in India, overseeing the production, quality, and withdrawal of unfit currency notes and coins from circulation. By ensuring a sufficient supply of good-quality currency, the RBI supports smooth financial transactions across the country.

- **Developmental Role**: The RBI undertakes promotional functions to support national goals. These include fostering financial inclusion, developing banking infrastructure in rural areas, and implementing various government schemes to promote economic growth.

- **Regulator of Payment and Settlement Systems**: To meet the country's needs, the RBI supervises and enhances secure payment systems. It oversees paper-based, electronic, and pre-paid payment instruments (e-wallets), mobile banking, ATM services, and online transactions, instilling public confidence in the country's payment and settlement framework.

- **Banker to the Government**: Acting as the central banker, the RBI manages the accounts of both central and state governments, performing merchant banking functions and facilitating government financial operations.

- **Banker to Banks**: The RBI maintains accounts for all scheduled banks, providing financial services, short-term borrowing, and facilitating interbank transactions, reinforcing its role as the "banker's bank."

5.2. Organizational Structure of the RBI

The RBI is overseen by the **Central Board of Directors**, appointed by the government, and led by the **Governor**, the bank's chief executive. The Central Board comprises 14 Directors representing various sectors (industry, agriculture, trade, and professions), one government representative (typically the Finance Secretary), and Directors from four Local Boards representing different regions of India. The Governor is supported by up to four Deputy Governors and a team of Executive Directors.

The RBI's mandate has expanded in recent years due to increased economic globalization. Its role in safeguarding financial stability has become more significant, involving close cooperation with domestic and international regulators to mitigate external economic shocks.

5.3. Significance of RBI's Role

The RBI's regulatory framework ensures the stability and efficiency of the Indian banking system, guiding the country's economic policies in alignment with global best practices. Through its multifaceted functions, the RBI not only stabilizes the currency but also encourages balanced economic growth, making it a cornerstone of India's financial ecosystem.

Chapter 6 Types of Banks

India's banking system is multifaceted, with different banks catering to various financial needs and population segments. Below are the primary types of banks in India, along with their unique characteristics and roles:

- **Central Bank**
  - **Overview**: The central bank, usually a nation's apex banking authority, oversees the banking system and ensures financial stability. It is called the "banker's bank" because it provides services to commercial banks and the government.
  - **Functions**: Controls monetary policy, regulates currency issuance, manages foreign exchange reserves, sets interest rates, and acts as the lender of last resort. In India, the Reserve Bank of India (RBI) is the central bank, governing other banks and implementing financial regulations.
- **Scheduled and Non-Scheduled Banks**
  - **Scheduled Banks**: Listed under the RBI Act, 1934, scheduled banks maintain a minimum paid-up capital of ₹5 lakh and are eligible for RBI support and privileges. They can further be categorized into:
    - **Public Sector Banks**: Majority government ownership; cater to social and priority sector objectives.
    - **Private Sector Banks**: Primarily owned by private entities and offer competitive, market-driven services.
    - **Foreign Banks**: Foreign-based banks with branches in India, mainly serving corporate clients.

- o **Regional Rural Banks (RRBs)**: Created to serve rural areas, especially for agricultural finance.
- o **Co-operative Banks**: Community-oriented, catering to the financial needs of specific groups through membership.
- **Non-Scheduled Banks**: Smaller banks not listed under the RBI Act, with limited privileges and less RBI oversight.

- **Public Sector Banks**
  - **Objective**: Primarily government-owned, these banks focus on social welfare, providing accessible services, and lending to priority sectors like agriculture and small businesses.
  - **Examples**: State Bank of India (SBI) and Union Bank of India.
  - **Sub-categories**:
    - o **SBI and Associates**: SBI and its regional affiliates, such as the State Bank of Patiala, operate under SBI branding.
    - o **Nationalized Banks**: Privately held banks that were nationalized to prevent monopoly and increase financial inclusivity.

- **Private Sector Banks**
  - **Overview**: These banks are privately owned, focused on profit, and typically provide services driven by market demand.
  - **Types**:
    - o **Old Private Sector Banks**: Established pre-nationalization and retained private ownership.
    - o **New Private Sector Banks**: Established post-1993 banking reforms to foster competition.

- **Foreign Banks**
  - **Role**: Foreign banks operate in India through branches or subsidiaries, offering specialized products like corporate loans, consumer finance, and international trade support.
- **Regional Rural Banks (RRBs)**
  - **Objective**: Established to provide banking services in rural areas, specifically to small farmers and rural artisans.
  - **Ownership**: Jointly held by the central government, state governments, and sponsoring public sector banks.
- **Co-operative Banks**
  - **Purpose**: Operate as cooperative societies, providing low-interest loans to members, primarily in rural areas.
  - **Types**:
    - **State Co-operative Banks**: Function at the state level.
    - **Central Co-operative Banks**: Serve districts and provide financial support to village-level societies.
    - **Primary Agricultural Credit Societies (PACS)**: Operate at the grassroots level, meeting local agricultural credit needs.
- **Specialized Banks**
  - Banks with a specific focus on serving distinct sectors or providing unique financial services:
  - **Types**:
    - **Investment Banks**: Facilitate capital-raising, mergers, and financial advisories.
    - **Industrial Banks**: Support industrial development with medium- and long-term finance.
    - **Retail Banks**: Focus on basic banking for individuals, offering savings accounts, deposits, and personal loans.

Shareholding pattern of Public Sector Banks including holding of Government of India, promoters other than the Government and other shareholders as on 31.3.2022

Bank	Shareholding as a % of total no. of shares		
	Promoter & Promoter Group		Public & others
	of which, Government of India (President of India)	of which, other than Government of India (President of India)	
Bank of Baroda	63.97%	0%	36.03%
Bank of India	81.41%	0%	18.59%
Bank of Maharashtra	90.97%	0%	9.03%
Canara Bank	62.93%	0%	37.07%
Central Bank of India	93.08%	0%	6.92%
Indian Bank	79.86%	0%	20.14%
Indian Overseas Bank	96.38%	0%	3.62%
Punjab National Bank	73.15%	0%	26.85%
Punjab & Sind Bank	98.25%	0%	1.75%
State Bank of India	57.59%	0%	42.41%
UCO Bank	95.39%	0%	4.61%
Union Bank of India	83.49%	0%	16.51%

Source: BSE limited

Chapter 7 Public Sector Unit

Definition: Public Sector Unit (PSU) banks, also known as public sector banks (PSBs), are financial institutions where the government owns a majority stake (more than 50%). This ownership provides the government with control and influence over the bank's operations and policies. In India, prominent PSU banks include the State Bank of India (SBI), Bank of Baroda, and Punjab National Bank (PNB), among others.

PSU banks hold significant value in India's economy due to their role in:

- **Financial Inclusion**: Expanding banking services to rural and underserved areas, fostering a more inclusive financial system.
- **Economic Development**: Supporting key economic sectors such as agriculture, small and medium enterprises (SMEs), and infrastructure, thereby driving overall growth.
- **Government Initiatives**: Acting as instruments to implement various government schemes, such as poverty alleviation, rural development, and social welfare programs.

7.1. Role

The role of PSU banks encompasses various responsibilities:

- **Custodians of Public Money**: Safeguarding public deposits and ensuring security for individual and business accounts.
- **Credit Extension**: Providing loans and credit to essential sectors to stimulate economic progress.

- **Financial Inclusion**: Focusing on incorporating unbanked and underbanked communities into the formal banking system.
- **Implementing Government Policies**: Acting as agents of government policies within the financial sector, ensuring alignment with national economic objectives.

Functions

The core functions of PSU banks include:

- **Deposit Mobilization**: Serving as a secure repository for public savings and deposits.
- **Lending**: Extending credit to individuals, businesses, and industries to facilitate economic activities.
- **Payment Services**: Providing essential payment and settlement services such as checks, demand drafts, and electronic funds transfers.
- **Investment**: Investing in government securities and other approved instruments to manage liquidity and earn returns.

Nature of Work

Commercial Banking: Engaging in traditional banking services such as deposit-taking, lending, and offering financial products.

- **Social Banking**: Committing to financial inclusion and uplifting marginalized communities, especially in rural areas.
- **Government Support**: Receiving government support, such as capital infusions, to ensure financial stability and reinforce their capital base when needed.

PSU banks in India are foundational to both economic and social development, providing vital financial services, supporting government programs, and fostering inclusive growth. Through a wide array of services, PSU banks not only drive economic activities but also help the government achieve policy goals aimed at enhancing welfare and promoting stability.

Chapter 8 Foreign and Private Banks

8.1. Foreign Banks: An Overview

Foreign banks in India are institutions headquartered in another country, with branches or representative offices in India. They originally entered India to support trade and business activities across Asia and the world.

Key historical entries:
- **Standard Chartered Bank**: Originally the Chartered Bank of India, it began operations in Calcutta in 1858 under a Royal Charter from Queen Victoria.
- **HSBC (Hong Kong and Shanghai Banking Corporation)**: Expanded into India in 1959 by acquiring Mercantile Bank.
- **BNP Paribas**: Initially operated as the Comptoir d'Escompte de Paris, beginning in 1860 in Calcutta, representing a significant French banking presence.
- **Citibank**: Known as The National City Bank of New York, it entered India in 1902 following the relaxation of U.S. banking laws prohibiting international branches.
- **JP Morgan**: Entered India in 1922 through a stake in Calcutta's Andrew Yule and Co. Ltd.

Today, foreign banks in India operate in two primary forms: foreign bank branches (46 banks as of December 14, 2023) and representative offices (34 banks).

8.2. Key Features of Foreign Banks

Foreign banks in India contribute significantly to the banking landscape, even with a limited number of branches.

- **Registration and Structure**
  - Foreign banks are headquartered abroad but operate branches within India.
  - They must comply with both Indian regulations (host country) and their home country's regulations.
  - Foreign branches often serve multinational clients and facilitate international business transactions.
- **Branch Network and Market Share**
  - While foreign banks comprise less than 1% of the total branch network, they control about 7% of total banking sector assets and account for approximately 11% of profits.
- **Regulatory Policy by the Reserve Bank of India (RBI)**
  The RBI's approach to foreign banks is based on two core principles:
  - **Reciprocity**: Foreign banks receive near-national treatment only if their home country permits Indian banks to operate branches freely.
  - **Single Mode of Presence**: Foreign banks in India must operate either as branches or as wholly owned subsidiaries (WOS), but not both.
- **Additional RBI Guidelines**
  Foreign banks in India must adhere to various regulatory requirements set by the RBI:
  - **Basel Standards**: They must maintain capital adequacy per the Basel regulatory framework.
  - **Minimum Capital Requirement**: Foreign banks must hold at least INR 500 crore in capital.
  - **Capital to Risk-weighted Assets Ratio (CRAR)**: A minimum CRAR of 10% is mandatory.

- **Priority Sector Lending**: 40% of foreign banks' lending must be allocated to the priority sectors defined by the RBI.

- **Representative Offices**
  Foreign banks may open representative offices as an entry point into the Indian market.
  - **Functionality**: Representative offices can establish client relationships and liaise between the parent bank and clients in India, but they cannot conduct direct banking transactions.
  - **Scope**: These offices allow foreign banks to assess and build relationships with potential clients while adhering to fewer regulatory requirements compared to full branches.

Foreign banks in India play an essential role in supporting international trade and providing global banking services to corporations and individuals. Despite their relatively small branch network, they hold substantial assets and profits within India's banking sector. Through careful regulatory oversight, the RBI ensures that foreign banks contribute to India's financial system while maintaining the balance between home and host country interests.

8.3. Private Banks: An Overview

Private banks in India are owned by private individuals or corporations, with a significant portion of their equity traded on the stock market. They are independent in terms of their financial strategies, while adhering to the regulatory guidelines set by the Reserve Bank of India (RBI). These banks are focused on providing better customer service and tailored solutions, and they operate with a profit-driven model.

Key Characteristics:

- **Ownership**: Private banks are primarily owned by private individuals or corporations, unlike public sector banks which are owned by the government.
- **Growth**: Private banks gained significant traction after the 1990s, particularly following the liberalization, privatization, and globalization (LPG) policy.
- **Market Presence**: Private banks tend to focus on urban areas and cater to a more affluent clientele, though they are expanding their services and reach to smaller towns and rural areas.

Types of Private Banks

Private sector banks in India are classified into two categories:

- **Old Private Sector Banks**: These are the banks that existed before 1968, during the period of nationalization.
- **New Private Sector Banks**: These emerged after the RBI issued guidelines in 1993 for the establishment of new private sector banks. Most of their shares are held by private entities, and they operate as limited liability companies.

As of April 1, 2024, there are 21 private banks in India.

Advantages of Private Banks:

- **Customer Focused**: Private sector banks are more responsive to customer needs and offer faster, more personalized services.
- **Tailored Financial Solutions**: They offer a wider range of products and services designed to meet individual customer financial goals.
- **Efficient Management**: The management systems of private banks are often more streamlined and efficient, enabling quicker decision-making.

- **Quick Financial Decisions**: Private banks are known for their agility in adapting to market changes and making financial decisions swiftly.

Disadvantages of Private Banks:

- **Higher Fees**: Private sector banks often charge higher fees for their services compared to public banks.
- **Urban-Centric Operations**: Private banks are mostly concentrated in urban areas, making them less accessible to rural populations.
- **Lack of Job Security**: Employees in private banks may face less job security compared to those in public sector banks.

Emergence and Growth

Private sector banks began to grow rapidly after the liberalization of the Indian economy in the 1990s. The introduction of new financial tools, cutting-edge technology, and innovative banking products allowed these banks to gain a competitive edge over public sector banks.

Notable Banks:

- **Axis Bank** and **IndusInd Bank** are among the oldest private banks in India, established in the early 1990s, when the government allowed private banks to operate more freely.

These banks have since established themselves as leaders in operational efficiency, innovation, and customer service.

Main Functions & Activities of Private Banks:

- **Deposit Mobilization**
  - **Savings Accounts**: Private banks attract deposits from individuals through savings accounts, offering competitive interest rates.

- **Fixed Deposits**: They offer fixed deposit schemes with flexible tenures and interest rates to cater to the needs of different depositors.
- **Lending and Credit Facilities**
  - **Personal Loans**: Private banks offer personal loans for various purposes, such as medical emergencies, education, or home renovations.
  - **Home Loans**: They provide financing options for individuals looking to purchase or construct homes.
  - **Business Loans**: Private banks offer credit facilities to businesses for working capital, expansion, or specific projects.
- **Wealth Management and Private Banking**
  - **Wealth Management Services**: These services are targeted at high-net-worth individuals, offering investment advisory, portfolio management, and estate planning.
  - **Private Banking**: Aimed at affluent clients, private banking services offer tailored financial solutions based on the client's specific needs.
- **Investment Banking**
  - **Underwriting**: Private banks may assist companies in raising capital through the issuance of stocks or bonds.
  - **Mergers and Acquisitions**: They provide financial advisory services for mergers, acquisitions, and corporate restructuring.
- **International Banking**
  - **Foreign Exchange Services**: Private banks facilitate international trade and investment by offering foreign exchange services for currency conversion and hedging.

- **International Remittances**: They offer remittance services for individuals and businesses with global connections.
- **Electronic Banking Services**
  - **Internet Banking**: Most private banks offer online platforms for customers to perform banking transactions, view account balances, and more.
  - **Mobile Banking**: Mobile banking apps enhance customer convenience, allowing banking on-the-go via smartphones.
- **Advisory Services**
  - **Financial Advisory**: Private banks provide comprehensive financial planning, helping clients manage investments, plan for retirement, and meet other financial goals.
  - **Risk Management**: Private banks assist clients in managing financial risks, offering insurance products and hedging strategies.
- **Corporate Banking**
  - **Working Capital Financing**: They offer working capital loans to businesses to support daily operations.
  - **Trade Finance**: Private banks provide services such as letters of credit and documentary collections to facilitate international trade.
- **Retail Banking**
  - **ATM Services**: Private banks maintain a vast network of ATMs to ensure customer access to cash and other banking services.
  - **Retail Products**: Private banks offer a range of retail banking products, including credit cards, debit cards, and other financial instruments tailored to meet individual needs.

Private banks in India play a pivotal role in the country's financial system, offering a wide array of services and products to meet the diverse needs of individual and corporate clients. Their rapid growth and innovative approach have positioned them as key players in the banking sector, particularly in urban areas. Despite their higher fees and urban-centric operations, private banks are known for their efficiency, customer service, and agility in adapting to market trends.

Chapter 9 NABARD and RRB

The need for institutional credit in rural India became evident early in the government's planning process. To boost the rural economy, the Reserve Bank of India (RBI) set up the Agricultural Refinance and Development Corporation (ARDC) in 1963. The ARDC's role was to provide refinancing support for development projects like irrigation, mechanization, and land development. However, various financial agencies offered fragmented credit support to different rural sectors, highlighting the necessity for a centralized institution that could handle all aspects of rural credit.

In 1979, the RBI set up a committee to Review the Arrangements for Institutional Credit for Agriculture and Rural Development (CRAFICARD), led by Shri B. Sivaraman, to recommend a unified approach. The committee's report underscored the need for a dedicated body that would focus on rural credit in a structured way. This recommendation led to the establishment of the National Bank for Agriculture and Rural Development (NABARD) in 1982, created under the NABARD Act, 1981. The functions of the RBI's Agricultural Credit Department (ACD), Rural Planning and Credit Cell (RPCC), and the ARDC were transferred to NABARD.

NABARD's primary role has been to oversee and promote rural development, with a special focus on agriculture. Based in Mumbai, NABARD has become India's apex banking institution for agriculture and rural development.

9.2. Functions of NABARD

The functions of NABARD can be categorized into three broad areas: **Credit Functions**, **Regulatory Functions**, and **Development Functions**.

Credit Functions:

- **Short-term Credit**: NABARD provides refinance assistance to state cooperative banks, sectoral rural banks, and other approved financial institutions for agricultural operations, marketing of agricultural products, and rural industries.
- **Medium-term Credit**: It offers loans with a minimum tenure of 18 months and a maximum of 7 years to state cooperative banks and Regional Rural Banks (RRBs).
- **Long-term Credit**: Loans are provided for periods up to 25 years to various banking institutions involved in rural development.
- **Special Credit Provisions**: NABARD offers special credit to support agricultural operations, artisan activities, and small-scale industries in rural areas, as well as providing credit during calamities like droughts.

Regulatory Functions:

- NABARD conducts inspections of cooperative societies (except primary cooperative societies) and RRBs to ensure sound banking practices.
- It monitors RRBs and cooperative banks' returns and ensures compliance with regulatory norms.
- NABARD plays a role in the integration of RRBs and cooperative societies into Core Banking Solutions (CBS),

enabling them to operate seamlessly across the banking network.

Development Functions:

- **Research and Development**: NABARD's R&D division promotes research on issues related to agriculture and rural development and assists in creating region-specific programs.
- **Training**: NABARD undertakes comprehensive training programs for agricultural and rural development personnel, helping enhance technical skills.
- **Support for Artisans**: The bank aids in marketing handicrafts and provides a platform for artisans to showcase their products.

NABARD has also formed partnerships with international organizations like the World Bank, which provides advisory and financial assistance for rural development and agricultural advancements.

9.3. Recent Changes in NABARD:

The **NABARD (Amendment) Bill, 2018** led to significant changes, including an increase in NABARD's authorized capital from ₹5,000 crore to ₹30,000 crore. The bill gives the Union Government the discretion to raise NABARD's capital depending on requirements, with the central government required to hold at least 51% of the share capital. Furthermore, the RBI transferred its share capital in NABARD, worth ₹20 crore, to the central government.

Additionally, the Bill has allowed NABARD to provide credit facilities to Micro, Small, and Medium Enterprises (MSMEs) in rural areas, with an investment of up to ₹20 lakh in machinery and plants, as well as extending credit to enterprises with investments up to ₹10 crore in the manufacturing sector and ₹5 crore in the services sector.

These amendments align with NABARD's ongoing efforts to support a broad spectrum of rural development initiatives, from agriculture to small and medium enterprises.

9.3 Contribution of NABARD to the Development of Rural Economy

NABARD has significantly contributed to the rural economy through its financial, developmental, and supervisory functions.

9.3.1 Financial Contribution:

- **Refinance**:
  - o **Short-Term Loans**: NABARD provides short-term loans to financial institutions for crop loans, ensuring food security in the country.
  - o **Long-Term Loans**: NABARD offers long-term refinancing options for financial institutions to support farm and non-farm activities, with loan tenors ranging from 18 months to over 5 years.
- **Rural Infrastructure Development Fund (RIDF)**:
  - o Set up in 1995-96 by RBI, it supports rural infrastructure projects by providing funds to financial institutions.
- **Long-Term Irrigation Fund (LTIF)**:
  - o Established in 2016-17 with a corpus of Rs 20,000 crore for irrigation development.

- **Pradhan Mantri Awaas Yojana – Grameen (PMAY-G)**:
  - o NABARD helps implement the PMAY-G for rural housing development.
- **NABARD Infrastructure Development Assistance (NIDA)**:
  - o NIDA complements RIDF to aid infrastructure development.
- **Warehouse Infrastructure Fund (WIF)**:
  - o Launched in 2013-14 with a corpus of Rs 5,000 crore, this fund provides loans to meet warehousing infrastructure needs for agricultural commodities.
- **Food Processing Fund**:
  - o NABARD provides financial support to promote food processing industries in rural areas.
- **Direct Lending to Cooperative Banks**:
  - o NABARD extends loans to cooperative banks for rural credit.
- **Credit Facility to Marketing Federations (CFF)**:
  - o Provides loans for rural marketing activities.
- **Producer Organizations Development Fund (PODF)**:

  - o Established with a corpus of Rs 50 crore to support Producer Organizations (POs) and Primary Agriculture Credit Societies (PACS) for multifaceted services.

- **Producer Organizations (PO)**:

  - o Legal entities formed by primary producers such as farmers, milk producers, artisans, etc., for profit-sharing among members.

- **Primary Agricultural Credit Society (PACS):**

  - Smallest co-operative credit institutions providing loans to farmers at the grassroots level.

9.3.2 Developmental Contribution:

- **Kisan Credit Card (KCC) Scheme:**
  - Launched in 1998, this scheme provides crop loans to farmers.
- **RuPay-Kisan Cards (RKCs):**
  - NABARD has helped rural financial institutions issue these cards to farmers, providing financial services.
- **Tribal Development:**
  - NABARD runs programs to promote development among tribal populations.
- **Climate Resilient Agriculture:**
  - Initiatives to ensure agricultural practices adapt to climate change.
- **Umbrella Programme on Natural Resource Management (UPNRM):**
  - Launched in 2007, this program focuses on improving rural investment and sustainable resource utilization.
- **Microfinance Sector:**
  - NABARD launched the **Self-Help Group-Bank Linkage Programme (SHG-BLP)** in 1992, linking millions of Self-Help Groups to credit.
- **E-Shakti:**
  - A digital initiative to digitize SHGs, launched in 2015.
- **Skill Development:**
  - Promotes rural entrepreneurship by encouraging the youth to start businesses in the rural off-farm sector.

- **Marketing Initiatives**:
  - Facilitates the participation of rural artisans and producers in exhibitions, improving their marketing reach.
- **Incubation Centres**:

  - NABARD supports Agri-Incubation Centres at agricultural universities like Chaudhary Charan Singh Haryana Agricultural University and Tamil Nadu Agricultural University, enabling innovation in agriculture.

9.4 Challenges Faced by NABARD

- **Loss of Link with RBI**:
  - The severing of ties between NABARD and RBI (due to the transfer of equity under the NABARD Act of 2017) has weakened the operational connection, impacting rural development and agriculture funding.
- **Increased Cost of Financing**:
  - With market borrowings accounting for 80% of NABARD's resources, the cost of financing has risen, impacting its ability to offer low-interest loans.
- **Low Credit Share for North-Eastern States**:
  - North-Eastern India receives a small portion of NABARD's credit allocation, which is insufficient to meet the needs of farmers in this region.
- **Credit Gaps in Rural Areas**:
  - While commercial banks are expected to cover credit gaps, the institutional credit provided by cooperative banks and NABARD remains critical for rural development.

9.5 Regional Rural Banks (RRBs)

RRBs were established in 1975 to improve the rural credit system and provide financial services to agricultural and non-agricultural sectors. They focus on vulnerable groups such as small and marginal farmers, agricultural labourers, and artisans. Initially established with the support of the Reserve Bank of India, RRBs have evolved as vital institutions for rural development by providing affordable loans and reducing dependence on moneylenders.

9.6 Significance of Regional Rural Banks (RRBs)

- **Operation as Commercial Banks**: RRBs offer loans and mobilize savings while targeting small and marginal farmers and rural artisans.
- **Priority Sector Lending (PSL)**: RRBs have a PSL target of 75%, ensuring they provide loans for agricultural and rural activities.
- **Financial Inclusion**: RRBs provide loans and financial services to regions and communities that commercial banks do not fully serve.

9.7 Limitations of RRBs

- **Financial Losses**: RRBs, on average, are losing money due to high operational costs and low-interest rates on small loans.
- **Loan Recovery Issues**: Loan recovery has been suboptimal, resulting in increasing debts.
- **Operational Challenges**: The cost of managing small loans is high, which reduces profitability.

Chapter 10 Nationalization of Banks

The nationalization of banks in India, particularly in 1969, is considered one of the most pivotal economic decisions in post-independence India. This major shift in policy was not just about transferring the ownership of banks to the government but was also deeply rooted in the broader socio-economic objectives of the time. Here's a detailed breakdown of the nationalization process, its driving forces, and its implications for India's banking system and economic development.

10.1 Nationalization in India

The nationalization of India's banking sector began in earnest in 1955 when the Imperial Bank of India was nationalized to create the **State Bank of India (SBI)**, which became the primary banking agent for the government. However, it was on **19th July 1969** that the government took the historic step of nationalizing 14 major commercial banks, an act that would go on to change the entire banking landscape of the country.

In the second phase, six more banks were nationalized in 1980, bringing 80% of India's banking sector under government control. This radical transformation occurred during a period of major socio-economic challenges in the country.

Factors Leading to Nationalization:

Several economic and political pressures led the Indian government to nationalize the banking sector:

- **Planned Economic Development**: After independence, India adopted a planned economic model aimed at fostering a socialistic society. Nationalization was seen as aligning with this policy of state control over major sectors of the economy.

- **Economic Shocks**: The country had suffered multiple shocks, including two wars (with China in 1962 and Pakistan in 1965) and two successive years of drought that severely impacted national food security. The reliance on food aid from the United States (PL 480 program) exposed vulnerabilities in India's economic structure.
- **Stagnant Economic Growth**: The 1960s and early 1970s saw India's economic growth stagnate. While the population grew, the per capita income remained almost flat. The economy was struggling, and the private sector banks were not adequately serving critical sectors like agriculture.
- **Agricultural Underfunding**: Between 1951 and 1968, the share of industrial credit disbursed by commercial banks increased, but agriculture received less than 2% of total bank credit. With the Green Revolution needing capital infusion for agricultural modernization, it became essential to redirect bank resources toward rural and agricultural development.
- **Social Welfare and Regional Imbalances**: Nationalization was also driven by the goal of addressing social welfare needs and reducing regional imbalances, especially the urban-rural divide. There was a push to bring banking services to rural areas and increase priority sector lending, which was critical for the agricultural economy.

10.2 Benefits of Nationalization

The nationalization of banks brought profound changes to the Indian banking landscape, some of which include:

- **Expansion of Banking Services**: Post-nationalization, the number of bank branches expanded dramatically, reaching remote areas that had been neglected before. The banking network grew by about 800% in terms of branches, making banking services accessible even in rural corners of India.

- **Increased Public Confidence**: With the government taking control of the banking sector, public confidence soared. People felt assured about the safety of their deposits, and trust in the banking system grew.

- **Economic Growth and Green Revolution**: Nationalized banks played a key role in financing the **Green Revolution** and supporting agricultural and rural development. This was pivotal in India's efforts to achieve food security and self-sufficiency.

- **Access to Credit for the Underprivileged**: Nationalization ensured that credit was no longer just available to large businesses or urban industries. Smaller industries, agriculture, and new entrepreneurs, particularly in backward areas, were given more opportunities to access credit.

- **Promotion of Social Goals**: One of the main objectives of nationalization was to drive **social welfare**, including prioritizing sectors like agriculture, small industries, and export-oriented businesses. The nationalized banks were also expected to support backward areas and reduce disparities between urban and rural regions.

- **Mobilization of Savings**: Nationalized banks were able to tap into the vast pool of savings in rural India, which were previously untapped or not efficiently mobilized. These savings were redirected into productive sectors, contributing to broader economic development.

- **Stabilizing the Banking Sector**: With government control, the banking sector was insulated from private monopolies and speculative practices. Public sector banks could focus on long-term development goals rather than short-term profits.

Challenges and the Shift Toward Liberalization

Despite these benefits, the post-nationalization period also had its challenges. By the late 1980s and early 1990s, the banking sector faced inefficiencies, mounting non-performing assets (NPAs), and political interference in lending decisions. The balance of payments crisis of 1991 prompted India to shift toward **liberalization, privatization, and globalization** (LPG reforms), with significant economic policy changes including banking sector reforms.

However, even after the liberalization of the early 1990s, the public sector banks continued to operate under significant government control, especially in terms of lending policies. The resulting NPAs became a critical issue, slowing down India's economic growth in the subsequent decades.

Nationalization in India was a pivotal policy decision that helped expand banking services to underserved regions, supported social and economic development goals, and ensured the mobilization of savings for productive purposes. However, it also set the stage for the inefficiencies that eventually led to calls for banking sector reforms in the post-1991 era. The evolution of India's banking sector reflects a delicate balance between state control and market dynamics, which continues to shape the country's financial landscape today.

The debate on the nationalization of banks in India, especially post-1969, is complex and multifaceted, with both positive and negative outcomes.

10.3 Was the Nationalization of Banks a Right Move?

Positive Aspects:

- **Credit Expansion to Priority Sectors:** The nationalization of banks aimed to improve access to credit for agriculture, small industries, and rural areas, which were under-served by private banks. This was crucial for creating new entrepreneurs and reducing regional economic disparities.
- **Wealth Redistribution:** Nationalization helped redistribute financial resources, making banking services more inclusive. It facilitated the growth of rural India and small-scale industries, contributing to the overall growth of the economy.

Negative Aspects:

- **Political Interference and NPA Crisis:** The nationalization of banks led to political interference in lending practices, which contributed to the credit bubble and, ultimately, the Non-Performing Assets (NPA) crisis. Political patronage often led to unsound loans being granted, resulting in high levels of NPAs, particularly after 2012.
- **Complex Interest Rate Structure:** Nationalization introduced a complex interest rate structure that was difficult for both banks and borrowers to navigate. This, in turn, led to inefficiency and a failure to channel loans to the most deserving sectors.
- **Bureaucratic Inefficiencies:** The nationalized banks, owing to their public sector status, became bureaucratic in nature. The lack of competition between public and private banks led to inefficiency, with delayed decision-making, red-tapism, and lack of accountability.

- **Weak Performance and High Overdue:** Nationalized banks faced challenges like economically unviable branches and a heavy burden of overdue loans, leading to long-term financial instability.

While the nationalization of banks aimed to promote financial inclusion and growth in rural sectors, the inefficiencies, political interference, and the NPAs crisis have undermined its success. Privatization might not be the immediate solution, but comprehensive governance reforms and resolution of NPAs are crucial.

10.4 Nationalization of the 1970s:

The 1970s and 1980s saw the emergence of structural inefficiencies due to nationalization policies:

- **Protectionism and Lack of Innovation:** The policy of nationalization, coupled with an inward-looking economy and the License Raj, stifled entrepreneurship and innovation. India missed out on globalization opportunities that could have spurred economic growth.
- **Fiscal Prudence Erosion:** Populist measures and rising government expenditure, without efficiency improvements, led to fiscal imbalances. There was an increase in subsidies and grants, resulting in a rise in non-productive government expenditure.
- **Decline in Exports:** India's exports declined significantly, reflecting the failure of protectionist policies in harnessing global market opportunities.

10.5 Present Impact:

- **Legacy of NPAs:** The NPA crisis of the public-sector banks is widely considered the legacy of the 1970s and 80s nationalization. Political pressure on banks to lend irresponsibly led to massive overdue loans, with public-sector banks facing a combined NPA of ₹5.47 lakh crore.
- **Declining Financial Health of PSBs:** The economic surveys point out that the financial position of public-sector banks (PSBs) has been poor, with low market value returns compared to private-sector banks.
- **Operational Challenges:** Public-sector banks suffer from "phone banking" (political influence on loan approvals) and lack the operational freedom necessary to make effective business decisions.
- **High Losses in the Insurance Sector:** Nationalization also contributed to inefficiencies in the insurance sector, with low penetration rates and poor financial health of public-sector insurers.

10.6 Role of Nationalization in Indian Economy:

Despite the challenges, nationalization led to several positive changes:

- **Bank Branch Expansion:** Bank branches in rural areas increased from 8,262 in 1969 to 30,303 in 1979, significantly improving banking accessibility.
- **Agriculture and Rural Growth:** The nationalization of banks contributed to the Green Revolution by providing increased credit to agriculture, reducing the exploitation of farmers by moneylenders.

- **Priority Sector Lending:** Banks began directing a substantial portion of credit (40%) towards agriculture, small-scale industries, housing, and weaker sections of society.
- **Economic Growth and Employment:** Nationalization led to increased domestic savings, investment, and employment, particularly in PSUs.

10.7 Achievements of Nationalization of Banks:

The nationalization of banks resulted in several positive outcomes, including:

- **Branch Expansion and Savings Mobilization:** Nationalized banks expanded their reach into rural areas, significantly increasing the mobilization of deposits and improving the accessibility of banking services.
- **Social Banking and Poverty Alleviation:** Banks played a key role in supporting government-led poverty alleviation programs.
- **Development of Priority Sectors:** The focus on priority sectors such as agriculture, small industries, and rural development contributed to balanced regional growth.

10.8 Criticism of Nationalization of Banks:

Despite the successes, nationalization faced significant criticisms:

- **Failure to Meet Objectives:** The original objectives of reducing regional disparities and providing adequate credit to priority sectors were not fully met. While loans increased, they were often insufficient to meet the demands of these sectors.

- **Regional Imbalances and Inefficiency:** The distribution of bank branches remained uneven across regions, with some areas remaining underserved.
- **Poor Profitability and Low Efficiency:** Many nationalized banks struggled with low profitability, inefficiency, and increasing NPAs due to political interference in lending.
- **Lack of Accountability:** Bureaucratic inefficiencies and political pressure contributed to the growth of NPAs, reducing the effectiveness of the banking sector.

Chapter 11 Expansion of Branches

The expansion of bank branches in India has been integral to the country's economic growth and development. It contributes significantly to financial inclusion, capital formation, and the accessibility of banking services, which are crucial for economic growth. Here is a detailed breakdown:

11.1 Role and Need:

- **Financial Inclusion**: The primary role of expanding bank branches is to promote financial inclusion. By establishing branches in underserved and rural areas, banks bring financial services to previously unbanked populations. This helps integrate a larger portion of society into the formal banking system, enabling them to access savings accounts, loans, and insurance products.
- **Access to Banking Services**: Expansion ensures that both individuals and businesses, especially in remote and rural areas, can access critical banking services. This includes opening accounts, obtaining loans, and engaging in day-to-day banking operations, all of which are necessary for personal and business growth.

11.2 Importance in the Economy:

- **Capital Formation**: Banks play a key role in capital formation by mobilizing savings from the public and directing them into investments that fuel economic activity. The growth of bank branches allows for a more efficient mobilization of these resources, fostering economic development.

- **Credit Disbursement**: The expansion of bank branches helps in the distribution of credit across various sectors, including agriculture, small businesses, and infrastructure. This credit is essential for economic expansion, job creation, and rural development.
- **Monetary Policy Transmission**: Banks serve as intermediaries in the implementation of monetary policies. By managing loans, deposits, and interest rates, bank branches help facilitate the central bank's policies and stabilize the economy.

11.3 Functions:

- **Deposit Mobilization**: One of the key functions of bank branches is to gather deposits. These deposits serve as the base from which loans and advances are made, thus supporting both consumer and business activities.
- **Lending**: Bank branches provide loans and advances to individuals, businesses, and other entities. This is essential for meeting various financial needs, ranging from personal loans to business financing.
- **Financial Advisory**: Bank branches also offer advisory services, helping customers make informed decisions about savings, investments, insurance, and loans. This guidance is crucial for promoting financial literacy and better money management.

11.4 Advantages:

- **Job Creation**: The establishment and expansion of bank branches create job opportunities, both directly within the banking sector (e.g., for tellers, loan officers, and managers) and indirectly in related sectors such as logistics, security, and retail.

- **Poverty Alleviation**: Expanding access to financial services to marginalized and economically weaker sections of society can help reduce poverty. By facilitating access to credit and savings, banks provide people with the tools to improve their livelihoods.
- **Infrastructure Development**: Bank branch expansions are often accompanied by infrastructure development. As banks establish their presence, they may contribute to building roads, improving communication networks, and boosting local infrastructure, which in turn benefits the broader community.

11.5 Factors Driving Expansion:

- **Government Initiatives**: Government policies such as the **Pradhan Mantri Jan Dhan Yojana (PMJDY)** have played a crucial role in expanding banking services to rural and underserved areas. These initiatives help promote financial inclusion and support the expansion of bank branches.
- **Technological Advancements**: The rapid growth of mobile banking, internet banking, and ATMs has made it easier and cost-effective for banks to reach remote areas. These technologies reduce the need for physical branches in every location, enabling banks to serve a wider audience.
- **Regulatory Support**: Regulatory bodies like the **Reserve Bank of India (RBI)** provide frameworks and incentives for banks to extend their services into underserved areas. By offering tax breaks, subsidies, or easing licensing requirements, the RBI helps foster branch expansion.

11.6 Challenges:

- **Infrastructure Challenges**: One of the primary hurdles in expanding bank branches is the lack of basic infrastructure, such as roads, electricity, and communication facilities, in rural and remote areas. This can make it difficult to establish and maintain physical branches.
- **Low Financial Literacy**: In many underserved areas, financial literacy remains low, which limits the ability of people to fully utilize banking services. Even if branches are established, customers may not understand how to use the available services, such as mobile banking, loans, or savings products. Educating people about financial services and their benefits is essential for increasing the usage of banking services.
- **Operational Costs**: Running branches in remote areas with fewer customers can be expensive. The operational costs of setting up branches, paying staff, and maintaining infrastructure may outweigh the benefits in the short term, which can limit the pace of expansion.
- **Cultural and Social Barriers**: In some regions, cultural factors or social biases may discourage people from engaging with formal banking services. Awareness campaigns and community engagement are necessary to overcome these barriers.

The expansion of bank branches in India plays a vital role in ensuring economic growth, financial inclusion, and the efficient functioning of the country's banking sector. While challenges such as infrastructure limitations and financial illiteracy persist, the benefits, including increased access to banking services, credit, and financial advice, far outweigh the drawbacks.

Chapter 12 Social Role of Banks

The role of banks and financial institutions in social empowerment and sustainable economic development has become increasingly essential. Banks not only contribute to the economic framework of a country but also play a critical role in societal upliftment and environmental sustainability. Below is a comprehensive overview of the key contributions of banks to these objectives.

Promoting Saving Habits

- Banks encourage people to save by offering various deposit schemes with attractive interest rates, which helps inculcate a saving culture among individuals and contributes to overall economic stability.

Channelling Funds to Productive Investments

- By mobilizing savings and directing these funds into productive sectors, banks facilitate capital formation, support industrial growth, and drive economic activities across sectors.

Capital Formation and Industrial Promotion

- Banks play a critical role in capital formation by accumulating deposits and providing loans to industries, thereby promoting entrepreneurship, industrial expansion, and economic diversification.

Facilitating Trade and Commerce

- Modern banking services like online banking, debit/credit cards, and mobile banking make transactions smoother, supporting trade and commerce both domestically and internationally.

Creating Employment Opportunities

- By fostering investments and industrial growth, banks indirectly contribute to job creation, addressing unemployment and enabling economic independence.

Supporting Agricultural and Rural Development

- Banks play a pivotal role in rural development by providing loans with lower interest rates for agriculture and rural businesses, thus supporting self-sufficiency and food security.

Implementing Monetary Policy

- Banks act as a tool for implementing monetary policy, aimed at stabilizing the economy against inflation, deflation, and other financial imbalances through lending activities and managing interest rates.

Achieving Balanced Development

- The spread of banking operations in rural and underserved areas supports balanced development, ensuring that rural communities have access to financial services for economic and social growth.

Risk Management in Economic Development

- Commercial banks act as risk assessors by evaluating loan applications, which reduces financial risk and promotes creditworthiness among borrowers. By managing lending risks, banks safeguard against financial instability.

Financing Small Businesses

- Banks support the growth of small businesses by providing loans that allow these enterprises to start, expand, and create employment. Small business growth contributes significantly to economic dynamism and job creation.

Encouraging Wealth Creation

- Banks offer various types of savings accounts, which help people build wealth over time. By collecting these deposits, banks can fund other businesses and individuals, fuelling investment and growth.

Supporting Government Spending and Deficit Financing

- Through the purchase of treasury bonds and other government securities, banks facilitate public spending and contribute to funding social programs, infrastructure, and public services.

Advancing Sustainable Development

- Beyond traditional financing, banks contribute to sustainable development by investing in green projects, promoting financial inclusion, and supporting climate-friendly policies. They act as communicators and educators on sustainability, encouraging clients to adopt environmentally responsible practices.

Setting Standards for Corporate Citizenship

- Banks hold the unique position to model and promote ethical practices in industries they finance. By advocating for sustainability and corporate responsibility, banks can influence positive social and environmental standards across sectors.

Addressing Systemic Risks and Encouraging Sustainable Investment

- By promoting impact-driven investment, banks help mitigate economic risks associated with climate change and environmental degradation, thereby supporting long-term economic resilience.

Banks have evolved to become crucial agents of social empowerment, sustainable economic development, and environmental responsibility. By addressing both economic needs and societal well-being, banks position themselves as vital components in shaping a more balanced, inclusive, and sustainable future.

Role of Commercial Banks in Economic Development

Commercial banks play a pivotal role in the economic development of any country, particularly by acting as financial intermediaries that drive capital formation, manage risk, and support both small businesses and government spending. The evolution of commercial banks has been significant, especially after independence, expanding to serve both conventional and non-conventional sectors.

Expansion in Non-Conventional Sectors

- Post-independence, Indian commercial banks have expanded their operations beyond traditional sectors to support non-conventional sectors. This shift from conservative banking has helped diversify India's economic growth and adapt to a planned economy.

Financial Intermediation

- Commercial banks in India, regulated by the Banking Regulation Act (1949), play a critical role as financial intermediaries. Through the lending process, they channel funds from savers to investors, stimulating economic activities across various sectors.

Risk Management

- Banks carefully assess potential borrowers to mitigate risk, evaluating credit scores, income, and debt levels. By identifying low-risk borrowers, banks minimize financial losses and strengthen the financial system.

Support for Small Businesses

- Banks finance small business ventures, which helps create employment opportunities and supports the economic development of regions. Commercial banks assist these businesses by providing start-up financing, enabling them to contribute significantly to employment and GDP growth.

Wealth Creation and Management

- Through various accounts, such as savings, checking, and certificates of deposit, banks enable individuals to build wealth. The deposits collected are then reinvested, promoting a cycle of economic growth and development.

Government Spending Support

- Commercial banks facilitate government operations by purchasing Treasury bonds, funding government programs, and supporting economic stability. This also enables deficit spending when necessary for development projects.

Sustainable Development and Social Impact

- Beyond traditional roles, banks today are key drivers of sustainable development. By leveraging their reach and networks, they promote social responsibility, climate change initiatives, and financial inclusion.

- Banks have adopted a shared-value approach where shareholder returns are balanced with positive social and environmental impacts. This broader responsibility aligns banks with global sustainability goals.

Education and Influence

- Banks educate the public and businesses on sustainability and climate change. They serve as bridges between scientific knowledge and societal needs, promoting awareness and action on pressing global issues.

Leadership in Corporate Citizenship

- By modelling sustainable practices, banks influence good corporate governance across sectors. Their leadership fosters a culture of accountability and sustainability within industries reliant on bank financing.

Attracting Sustainable Investments

- Banks encourage institutional investors to fund ventures that promise both returns and societal benefits, thereby steering investments toward sustainable development.

The unique position of commercial banks within the economy allows them to not only support growth through financing but also to inspire transformative social and environmental change, making them indispensable to economic development and sustainable progress.

UNIT II LENDING DYNAMICS IN BANKING

Chapter 13 Priority Sector Lending

Origin and Development of Priority Sector Lending

- The concept of PSL traces back to the **1967-68 Credit Policy** when commercial banks were encouraged to finance priority sectors such as agriculture, exports, and small-scale industries.
- In **1971**, the RBI constituted an **Informal Study Group** to define priority sectors, leading to modified PSL guidelines in **1972**.

Objective of Priority Sector Lending

- **PSL** aims to ensure that certain economically crucial sectors receive adequate credit to support their development, which may otherwise be overlooked by the banking system.

Categories of Priority Sectors

- **Agriculture**: Includes loans for crop production, allied sectors, and agricultural infrastructure.
- **Micro and Small Enterprises (MSEs)**: Loans for manufacturing, services, and small businesses.
- **Education**: Financing for individuals pursuing higher education and educational institutions.
- **Housing**: Loans for residential construction within specified limits.
- **Renewable Energy**: Loans for solar, wind, and other renewable projects.
- **Others**: Includes export credit, social infrastructure, and loans to weaker sections like small farmers, scheduled

castes, scheduled tribes, and beneficiaries under government schemes.

Targets and Monitoring

- Banks are mandated by the **RBI** to allocate a percentage of their credit to PSL sectors and regularly report compliance.
- The RBI sets **specific targets** and monitors bank performance, with potential penalties for non-compliance.

Advantages and Objectives of PSL

- **Inclusive Growth**: Supports credit flow to underserved sectors and promotes rural and inclusive development.
- **Rural Development**: Emphasizes agriculture financing and infrastructure in rural areas.
- **Employment Generation**: Encourages entrepreneurship through loans to small enterprises, fostering economic activity and job creation.
- **Social Development**: Addresses housing and education, helping enhance living standards and access to quality education.

Challenges and Criticisms

- **Compliance Challenges**: Economic conditions or limited local opportunities can make it difficult for banks to meet PSL targets.
- **Risk Management**: Certain PSL sectors come with higher risks, necessitating robust risk management.
- **Impact on Profitability**: Concessional interest rates for PSL loans may impact bank profits.

Impact of Nationalization on PSL

- **1969 Bank Nationalization**: With the nationalization of banks, the Indian banking system was reoriented to support PSL more actively, leading to better access to credit for small borrowers, especially in rural areas.
- This led to increased bank involvement in socially important sectors, with a focus on providing institutional credit at reasonable rates.

Revised Definitions of Weaker Sections

- Priority sectors include specific groups such as:
  - **Small and marginal farmers**
  - **Artisans and cottage industries**
  - **Beneficiaries under schemes like Swarnajayanti Gram Swarojgar Yojana (SGSY)**
  - **Scheduled Castes and Tribes**

Broad Categories of Priority Sector Advances

- **Agriculture (Direct and Indirect)**: Loans to individual farmers, SHGs, JLGs, and related entities up to Rs. 20 lakhs.
- **Small-Scale Industries (Direct and Indirect)**: Loans for manufacturing, processing, and preservation by SSI units.
- **Small Business/Service Enterprises**: Loans for small business, retail trade, and various professional enterprises.
- **Micro Credit**: Financial services for poor borrowers, not exceeding Rs. 50,000.
- **Education Loans**: Loans up to Rs. 10 lakhs for studies in India and Rs. 20 lakhs for studies abroad.
- **Housing Loans**: Loans up to Rs. 15 lakhs for housing, with additional stipulations for repairs in rural and urban areas.

Non-Performing Assets (NPAs) in Priority Sector

- PSL contributes significantly to **NPAs** in public sector banks, especially in agriculture and other sectors with high credit risk.
- NPA trends in PSL remained high between 44% and 52% for public sector banks, with fewer NPAs for foreign banks due to their lower PSL commitments.

Major Issues in PSL

- **Low Profitability**: PSL mandates, along with pre-emption of funds and low-interest loans, contribute to reduced profitability.
- **High NPAs**: Higher default rates are observed, especially in sectors with weak repayment capabilities.
- **Quantitative Targets**: Fixed targets may pressure banks into indiscriminate lending without regard to borrower risk.
- **Government Interference**: Government policies and interventions may skew lending in Favor of large borrowers, reducing support to weaker sections.
- **Transaction Costs**: Administering many small loans is labour-intensive, increasing operational costs and affecting service quality.

Chapter 14 Base Rate and Prime Lending Rate

In recent years, India's financial sector has undergone significant reforms, allowing banks more flexibility in setting interest rates, provided they comply with RBI guidelines. Banks can adjust interest rates independently, though they must consider the RBI's frameworks like the Prime Lending Rate System and the Benchmark Prime Lending Rate (BPLR) to ensure that rates are competitive across institutions. The introduction of the Base Rate, among other regulatory measures, has marked a major step in this transformation.

The Base Rate is defined as the minimum lending rate established by the RBI, beneath which banks in India are not permitted to extend credit to clients, barring any special mandates from the government. Launched in June 2010, the Base Rate serves as the standardized lending rate provided by commercial banks, aiming to increase transparency and ensure that borrowers benefit from reduced interest rates. Banks determine their lending rates by adding a reasonable margin to the Base Rate, factoring in the borrower's credit risk profile. The Base Rate, set by the RBI, aims to harmonize lending rates across Indian banks, both public and private. Its calculation includes common components across borrower classes, such as the cost of deposits, administrative expenses, the bank's profitability over the past fiscal year, and various other operational costs. Banks may use diverse deposit tenures in Base Rate calculations, with the greatest weight given to the cost of deposits.

The factors that determine the Base Rate in India include:

- The cost of funds, including interest paid on deposits

- Operating expenses borne by the bank
- Minimum required returns
- Cash Reserve Ratio (CRR) costs

Differences in these elements, particularly deposit rates, contribute to varying Base Rates across banks. Although the Base Rate was once the lowest permissible lending rate, it was replaced in April 2016 by the Marginal Cost of Funds Based Lending Rate (MCLR), which introduced a more dynamic and transparent approach to interest rate determination. All loans sanctioned post-April 2016 are governed by the MCLR, shifting away from the Base Rate framework.

The Prime Lending Rate (PLR) serves as a benchmark interest rate for banks' most creditworthy borrowers. As the minimum rate offered to highly reliable clients, such as large corporations and financial institutions, it influences interest rates on various loans and credit facilities. PLR calculation involves each bank assessing the cost of funds, operational expenses, and lending risk for its most reliable clients. As a reference rate, other loan rates are often determined by adding or subtracting a margin from the PLR. It typically applies to large corporate borrowers with strong financial credentials. The PLR encompasses a risk premium to cover potential default risks and adjusts periodically to reflect economic shifts and changes in the cost of funds. Influenced by broader economic conditions and the central bank's monetary policy, the PLR has historically impacted lending rate structures. While the PLR has been phased out in some jurisdictions, the understanding of its historical relevance aids in comprehending how banks set interest rates and manage risk.

Since April 2016, the RBI has mandated the Marginal Cost of Funds Based Lending Rate (MCLR) as the standard benchmark for lending rates in Indian banks, encouraging more timely and transparent rate adjustments. The MCLR, calculated monthly, factors in the marginal cost of funds, including the repo rate, fund costs, and operational expenses. Components of the MCLR include:

- Marginal Cost, which considers borrowing costs, net worth returns, and marginal funding returns
- Operational costs necessary for bank operations
- Negative Carry-on CRR, which accounts for costs associated with maintaining required reserves with the RBI

Banks must review and reset their MCLR at least monthly, allowing quick adaptation to changing fund costs. The MCLR structure comprises tenor-linked rates, typically ranging from overnight to one-year durations, enabling borrowers to align loans with suitable tenors. Loans are priced by adding a spread to the MCLR, determined by the borrower's credit risk and financial health. This pricing model facilitates the transmission of policy rate adjustments to lending rates, enhancing the impact of monetary policy on economic growth.

The MCLR also marked a departure from the Base Rate, with new loans linked to the MCLR since April 1, 2016, while pre-existing loans remain under the Base Rate until maturity. Additionally, the RBI introduced guidelines requiring new retail and small business loans to be linked to external benchmarks, such as the repo rate, to boost transparency and transmission efficiency. The RBI periodically reviews the MCLR framework to ensure its relevance and alignment with India's economic landscape.

Chapter 15 Deposit Mobilization

Deposit mobilization in banking is the process banks use to attract funds from individuals, businesses, and institutions in the form of deposits. This activity is essential for banks as deposits form a stable source of funding, fuelling their lending, investment, and liquidity management. Effective deposit mobilization supports not only the bank's profitability but also the broader economic environment by fostering financial intermediation and liquidity in the market.

Types of Deposits

- **Demand Deposits**: These accounts allow customers to withdraw funds without notice, ensuring liquidity. Current accounts, typically used by businesses for transactional purposes, are a primary example of demand deposits.
- **Time Deposits**: Unlike demand deposits, time deposits require a commitment from depositors to leave funds in the bank for a fixed period. Examples include fixed deposits and recurring deposits, which often offer higher interest rates than demand deposits as a reward for depositor loyalty.

Methods of Deposit Mobilization

- **Branch Network Expansion**: Banks increase their geographical presence through branches, especially in underserved regions. Branches play a crucial role in reaching new customers, fostering relationships, and making banking more accessible to diverse communities.
- **Digital Banking Channels**: Modern banks leverage online and mobile banking to offer convenient services, from account management to competitive interest rates. Digital

platforms simplify deposit transactions, enabling customers to access their funds and manage their accounts anytime.

- **Marketing and Advertising**: Banks employ advertising campaigns across various media, promoting attractive interest rates, rewards, and exclusive offers. These marketing efforts help banks build brand awareness and attract new depositors.
- **Relationship Management**: Developing and nurturing customer relationships is essential in deposit mobilization. Through personalized service and dedicated relationship managers, banks strive to understand and cater to the specific financial needs of customers, enhancing loyalty and retention.

Role and Importance of Deposit Mobilization

- **Primary Source of Funds**: Deposits represent a critical funding base for banks, enabling them to finance loans and investments. A stable deposit base supports economic growth by facilitating the availability of credit to businesses and individuals.
- **Liquidity Management**: Deposits provide liquidity, ensuring that banks have readily available funds to meet withdrawal requests, manage cash flow, and handle other short-term obligations. Maintaining sufficient liquidity also supports depositor confidence and the bank's reputation.
- **Foundation for Lending**: Deposits are the backbone of a bank's lending capability, allowing them to channel funds from savers to borrowers. This process is vital to economic activity as it enables credit for investments, business operations, and personal needs.
- **Revenue Generation Through Interest Income**: By lending deposited funds at a margin, banks earn interest,

which forms a significant portion of their revenue. This income directly impacts the bank's profitability, allowing it to reinvest in its operations and expand services.

- **Support for Investment Initiatives**: The funds collected through deposits are often allocated to investments in various sectors such as infrastructure, real estate, and public services. This investment contributes to long-term economic growth and development.
- **Financial Stability**: A well-mobilized deposit base strengthens the bank's resilience during economic downturns and unexpected financial shocks. Stable deposits serve as a cushion, supporting the bank's balance sheet and helping it weather adverse economic conditions.
- **Interest Rate Influence**: The volume of deposits directly impacts interest rates. A higher deposit base enables banks to offer lower lending rates, which benefits borrowers. Conversely, limited deposits can result in higher interest rates as banks compete for funds.
- **Promotion of Savings**: Banks encourage saving habits by offering attractive deposit schemes, contributing to the financial discipline of customers. This culture of saving not only benefits individuals but also builds a larger pool of funds that can be channelled back into the economy.
- **Alignment with Monetary Policies**: Deposit mobilization levels help central banks gauge money supply and credit conditions, which inform policy decisions. For example, higher deposits might signal economic stability, enabling more lenient monetary policies.
- **Innovation in Financial Products**: In their quest to attract deposits, banks often create innovative savings and investment products tailored to diverse customer needs. This innovation provides customers with greater flexibility and more options in managing their finances.

- **Risk Mitigation**: A diverse and extensive deposit base reduces a bank's dependency on any single funding source, lowering financial risk. This diversification helps banks manage liabilities and protect against market uncertainties.
- **Local Economic Development**: By mobilizing deposits from local communities, banks play a direct role in economic development at the grassroots level. Funds from these deposits are often reinvested in the same communities through loans to small businesses, housing projects, and community development initiatives.

Deposit mobilization thus serves as a foundational aspect of banking, ensuring that banks have the necessary resources to support economic activity, maintain stability, and foster financial inclusivity. Through various deposit products and methods, banks work to build strong relationships with their customers, providing essential financial services and contributing to the growth of the financial sector and the economy.

Chapter 16 Composition of Banks deposits and lending

The **loan-to-deposit ratio (LDR)** is a key indicator of a bank's liquidity, assessing how effectively a bank uses its deposits to extend loans. Calculated as a ratio of total loans to total deposits, the LDR provides insight into the bank's balance between lending and available reserves. Maintaining an optimal LDR is crucial because it reflects a bank's ability to meet withdrawal demands and manage unforeseen financial needs, while also highlighting its potential for generating revenue from loans. Here's an in-depth analysis of the LDR and the role of deposit and loan composition in bank financial management:

16.1. Loan-to-Deposit Ratio (LDR)

LDR=Total Loans / Total Deposits

Purpose of LDR:

- The LDR measures the percentage of deposits being used to fund loans, indicating how much of a bank's deposit base is actively generating revenue.
- It's a crucial metric for liquidity management, helping banks ensure they have enough cash reserves while maximizing income from interest on loans.

16.2. Implications of High and Low LDR:

- **High LDR (Over 100%)**: A bank with an LDR over 100% has loaned more than it has in deposits, potentially indicating a liquidity shortfall if sudden withdrawal demands arise. High LDR can also increase reliance on external borrowing, which adds costs and can compress profit margins.

- **Low LDR**: An LDR far below the optimal range may indicate under-utilization of deposits. This conservative approach might result in missed revenue opportunities, as the bank is not fully leveraging its deposit base for profitable lending.

Role of the Loan-to-Deposit Ratio

- **Liquidity and Stability**: LDR is a direct measure of a bank's capacity to fulfil its obligations to depositors and absorb loan losses. During economic downturns, banks with balanced LDRs are better positioned to maintain stability and withstand loan defaults.
- **Attracting and Retaining Customers**: Rising deposits reflect the bank's success in attracting and maintaining a customer base. A robust deposit inflow enables banks to lend without relying on costly debt financing.
- **Interest Cost Management**: Unlike deposits, borrowing to fund loans incurs interest expenses. High LDRs may signal a need for the bank to take on debt, reducing profitability since borrowing costs are typically higher than the interest paid on deposits.
- **Investment Analysis**: For investors, the LDR serves as a barometer of a bank's financial health, with an ideal LDR indicating a strong balance between profitability and risk management. A well-managed LDR signals that the bank has sufficient deposits to fund loans without excessive reliance on external debt.

Ideal LDR Range

- **Optimal LDR**: The LDR sweet spot often falls between **80% and 90%**. At this range, the bank uses a significant portion of deposits for lending while maintaining enough reserves for liquidity.

- **Regulatory Influence**: Regulatory bodies may impose guidelines on LDR levels to ensure banks maintain adequate reserves. This regulatory oversight ensures banks remain solvent, thereby promoting financial stability.

Limitations of the Loan-to-Deposit Ratio

While LDR is a valuable indicator of a bank's liquidity and lending efficiency, it has limitations:

- **Loan Quality Assessment**: LDR only reflects the volume of loans relative to deposits, not the quality of those loans. High-risk loans could jeopardize stability despite an ideal LDR.
- **Defaulted Loans**: The ratio does not account for loans in default or arrears, meaning it may overstate liquidity if there is a significant portion of non-performing loans.
- **Comparative Context**: LDR is most informative when analysed alongside other banks of similar size, market, and lending strategy. Banks serving different customer demographics may have varying LDRs based on their customer needs and risk tolerance.

16.3. Composition of Bank Deposits

The structure of deposits influences a bank's stability and lending strategy. Banks attract a range of deposits that serve as the foundation for lending and liquidity management.

- **Savings Deposits**: Individuals commonly hold these for personal savings, offering moderate interest with some restrictions. They're a stable source of funds due to low volatility and predictable withdrawals.

- **Current (Checking) Deposits**: Used mainly by businesses, these accounts provide high liquidity but generally do not earn interest. They facilitate daily financial transactions, including payroll and expenses.
- **Fixed (Time) Deposits**: Depositors commit funds for a set period in exchange for higher interest. These deposits help banks forecast available funds and provide stable, long-term financing for lending.
- **Recurring Deposits**: Customers deposit a fixed amount regularly, accumulating savings over time. These deposits offer banks a reliable, growing source of funds to support predictable, medium-term lending needs.
- **Certificates of Deposit (CDs)**: CD accounts provide fixed-term deposits at premium interest rates. Often attracting institutional funds, CDs diversify a bank's deposit structure and appeal to clients seeking stable returns.
- **Foreign Currency Deposits**: Held in non-domestic currencies, these deposits allow customers to safeguard against currency fluctuations. They cater to clients engaged in international trade and contribute to a bank's diversified deposit base.

16.4. Composition of Bank Lending

Understanding loan types helps banks' balance risk, profitability, and alignment with customer needs. Banks manage a portfolio of diverse loan products, each serving distinct market segments:

- **Consumer Loans**: Personal loans, auto loans, and credit card loans fall under this category. Typically unsecured, these loans are subject to higher interest rates and fees, providing significant income.

- **Mortgage Loans**: Secured by real estate, mortgage loans are a major lending area for banks. Mortgages offer a stable, long-term income stream and can be sold on secondary markets, enhancing liquidity.
- **Business Loans**: Ranging from term loans to trade finance, these loans support business growth, daily operations, and expansion. Business loans are typically secured, although credit terms vary.
- **Government and Municipal Loans**: Provided to public entities, these loans fund infrastructure projects and community initiatives. Banks benefit from reduced default risk, as such loans are backed by government guarantees.
- **Small Business Loans (SMEs)**: Tailored for small and medium-sized enterprises, these loans address operational and expansion needs. Banks may offer flexible terms to support SME growth, stimulating local economies.
- **Educational and Student Loans**: Offered to individuals for educational expenses, these loans support human capital development. Repayment often begins post-graduation, providing banks a stable but deferred income source.
- **Agri-Business Loans**: Structured for agricultural needs, these loans align with the crop cycle and seasonal income fluctuations, supporting farmers and agribusinesses.

16.5. Importance of Deposit and Loan Composition

The deposit and lending structure are crucial for banks to manage risk, allocate resources effectively, and meet regulatory requirements. A well-balanced deposit base provides a low-cost, stable source of funding, while diversified lending enables banks to mitigate risk, capture market opportunities, and maximize returns. Both deposit and lending activities can shift based on economic conditions, regulatory requirements, and individual bank strategies.

LDR and deposit-lending composition are central to a bank's operational stability and financial health, shaping how it manages liquidity, mitigates risk, and serves its clientele. Banks continuously monitor these metrics to align their strategies with economic cycles, regulatory expectations, and profitability goals, ultimately contributing to a stable and resilient banking sector.

Chapter 17 Consortium of banks

A banking consortium is an alliance of two or more banks that collaborate to provide significant funding or financial services to a single borrower or group of borrowers. This partnership enables banks to pool resources, diversify risk, and expand market reach, especially for projects that require extensive capital and exceed the lending capacity of a single bank. Consortium financing is particularly essential for large projects or loans involving complex risk profiles, such as infrastructure developments, mergers, and acquisitions, and significant corporate transactions.

17.1. Purpose of a Banking Consortium

Banking consortia provide various benefits and are typically formed for several reasons:

- **Risk Mitigation**: By distributing financial exposure across multiple institutions, each bank in the consortium bears a portion of the risk rather than absorbing it fully. This risk-sharing is particularly important for large, potentially volatile projects and lowers the probability of a significant impact on any single bank's balance sheet.
- **Larger Financial Transactions**: Large-scale projects often require more capital than individual banks are willing or able to lend. A consortium structure enables banks to collectively finance projects beyond their individual lending limits, ensuring that clients receive the required funds.
- **Diversification of Expertise**: Member banks bring varied expertise, insights, and industry-specific knowledge, enhancing risk assessment and project evaluation. This

collective knowledge benefits the consortium, particularly in specialized sectors like energy, construction, or technology.

- **Pooling Resources**: Consortia pool resources, including capital and specialized financial services, which boosts their ability to support capital-intensive projects. This pooling maximizes loan size and enables banks to undertake deals that align with both their financial and strategic interests.

- **Enhanced Market Access**: A consortium allows banks to access different markets and clients, especially when individual banks have limited geographical reach or local expertise. Through collaboration, banks can expand their market presence and portfolio diversification.

- **Facilitation of Syndicated Loans**: Banking consortia often facilitate syndicated loans, wherein multiple banks provide funding under a single loan facility. In such cases, one bank acts as the lead arranger, streamlining loan administration and simplifying borrower relations by centralizing coordination.

- **Project Finance and Infrastructure Development**: Large-scale projects, such as infrastructure, require substantial funding and long-term commitment. Consortia are ideal for financing these projects, as they enable resource sharing and mitigate risks associated with construction, market fluctuations, or regulatory shifts.

- **Regulatory Compliance**: Regulatory limits often restrict individual banks from overexposing themselves to single borrowers or sectors. By sharing exposure across a consortium, each bank stays within regulatory guidelines, allowing them to pursue larger projects without violating compliance rules.

- **Flexible Funding Structures**: Consortia allow for flexible loan structures, where different banks may participate in varying portions or tranches. This flexibility enables the consortium to create funding models that meet the borrower's needs while aligning with each bank's risk tolerance and strategic goals.

- **Economies of Scale**: Collaborating in a consortium enables banks to streamline due diligence, legal documentation, and administrative processes, leading to economies of scale. By sharing responsibilities and costs, consortium members can reduce operational expenses.

17.2. Procedure Involved in a Banking Consortium

The procedure for forming and operating a banking consortium follows a series of structured steps:

- **Assessment of the Proposal**: The borrower presents a financing proposal to an initial bank, which evaluates the project's feasibility, financial stability, and associated risks. If approved, the lead bank reaches out to other banks to form the consortium.

- **Selection of Consortium Participants**: The lead bank selects banks with the requisite financial capacity, industry expertise, and appetite for exposure. These banks assess the proposal independently to determine their interest and the portion of the loan they are willing to finance.

- **Documentation and Verification**: Member banks verify the borrower's documentation, including project plans, financial records, and collateral, ensuring compliance and the validity of claims. This step is critical to safeguard against financial misrepresentation.

- **Exchange of Credit Information**: Consortium members exchange credit information, either from the borrower's previous banks or through credit bureaus, providing insight into the borrower's credit history and financial behavior.

- **Consortium Agreement**: Upon finalizing assessments and approving participation, the consortium members sign a formal consortium agreement that outlines their respective roles, contributions, and responsibilities. This agreement specifies the terms for resource sharing, decision-making, and risk management.

17.3. Differences Among Loan Syndication, Multiple Banking Arrangement, and Consortium

Although loan syndication, multiple banking arrangements, and banking consortia may seem similar, they serve distinct purposes and structures.

- **Loan Syndication**:
  - Involves a group of banks funding a single large loan to a borrower, with a lead bank (arranger) coordinating the loan.
  - The lead bank negotiates loan terms with the borrower, administers the loan, and often retains a portion of it while syndicating the remainder to other banks.
  - The syndicate may have decision-making protocols where major changes require member approval. Syndication provides flexibility, as each bank can choose its level of participation.
- **Multiple Banking Arrangement**:
  - In this arrangement, a borrower receives financing from multiple banks independently without a coordinated structure.
  - Each bank negotiates individually with the borrower, conducting due diligence, arranging documentation, and structuring terms independently.

- o There is no lead bank, no collective agreement, and less inter-bank coordination. Each bank assumes responsibility for its portion, with no risk-sharing or centralized decision-making.
- **Banking Consortium**:
  - o A consortium is a formal collaboration among banks that extends beyond a single loan, typically involving joint funding, shared risk, and pooled resources.
  - o Consortia agreements can involve a lead bank or equal collaboration, depending on the terms. Consortium members often share decision-making responsibilities, administrative tasks, and risk mitigation strategies.
  - o Consortia can support a variety of financial activities, including project finance and infrastructure, offering banks a platform for joint efforts across multiple deals.

17.4. Key Considerations in Banking Consortia

To ensure the successful operation of a banking consortium, banks must address the following considerations:

- **Strategic Alignment**: Banks should ensure that their strategic goals align with the consortium's objectives. This alignment fosters a collaborative environment and facilitates consensus-building.
- **Risk Assessment and Monitoring**: Consortia require robust risk assessment and monitoring frameworks to manage collective exposure. Banks must continuously monitor project developments, borrower performance, and market conditions.
- **Effective Communication**: Clear communication protocols are essential for coordination among members. Transparent

communication helps in quick decision-making, conflict resolution, and maintaining trust among consortium banks.

- **Consortium Management**: The lead bank, if appointed, must efficiently coordinate consortium activities. Effective management includes scheduling meetings, ensuring compliance, and enforcing adherence to the consortium agreement.
- **Exit Strategy**: Consortia must have an exit strategy for member banks, particularly if a bank decides to withdraw from the agreement. An exit strategy provides clarity and prevents disruptions to the consortium's operation.

Banking consortia play a critical role in the financial industry by enabling banks to engage in transactions that require substantial capital and shared risk. Through collaboration, consortia help banks expand their market reach, diversify portfolios, and participate in large-scale development initiatives that support economic growth and financial stability.

Chapter 18 Nonperforming Asset – Issues and Remedies

Definition of NPAs

Non-Performing Assets, or NPAs (often referred to as "bad loans"), are loans where the borrower fails to repay either interest or principal on time. In India, the RBI classifies a loan as an NPA if it remains unpaid for over 90 days.

18.1. Causes of NPAs

- **Economic Downturn**: Economic slowdowns lead to business failures, resulting in loan defaults.
- **Sectoral Issues**: Sectors like infrastructure, power, and steel face challenges that lead to NPAs.
- **Corporate Governance**: Poor governance within borrower companies contributes to non-repayment.
- **Policy and Regulatory Factors**: Government policy shifts or regulatory changes can affect borrowers' financial health.

18.2. Impact of NPAs on Banks

- **Erosion of Profits**: NPAs decrease bank profitability as banks lose expected interest income and must allocate provisions.
- **Capital Erosion**: Provisioning for NPAs eats into a bank's capital base, affecting lending abilities.
- **Reduced Lending Capacity**: High NPAs make banks more risk-averse, reducing their willingness to extend credit.
- **Higher Borrowing Costs**: To offset NPA losses, banks may increase loan interest rates, impacting borrowing costs across the economy.

- **Negative Market Perception**: High NPAs can harm a bank's stock price and credit rating.
- **Operational Challenges**: Managing NPAs involves legal proceedings, recovery efforts, and resource allocation, impacting regular banking operations.
- **Systemic Risk**: If widespread, NPAs pose a threat to the financial system, potentially triggering economic instability.

18.3. Management of NPAs

- **Early Detection**: Regular monitoring of borrower financial health helps in identifying and addressing potential NPAs.
- **Due Diligence and Credit Appraisal**: Rigorous evaluation of borrowers' business models and market conditions can prevent future NPAs.
- **Restructuring and Rescheduling**: Loan terms can be adjusted to aid borrowers facing temporary financial challenges.
- **Loan Recovery and Collection**: Banks work on active loan recovery through negotiation, repayment plans, and legal actions.
- **Asset Reconstruction**: Banks transfer NPAs to Asset Reconstruction Companies (ARCs) to clean up balance sheets and improve financial health.
- **Insolvency and Bankruptcy Code (IBC)**: IBC in India provides a legal structure for resolving insolvencies in a time-bound manner.

18.4. Types of NPAs in India

- **Substandard Assets**: Loans overdue for less than 12 months.

- **Doubtful Assets**: Loans overdue for over 12 months, with uncertain recovery.
- **Loss Assets**: Assets identified as having little recovery potential.
- **Special Mention Accounts (SMA)**: Loans showing early signs of distress:
    - **SMA-0**: 1-30 days overdue
    - **SMA-1**: 31-60 days overdue
    - **SMA-2**: 61-90 days overdue
- **Standard Assets**: Regularly repaid loans.
- **Restructured Standard Assets**: Loans with adjusted terms for borrowers facing financial difficulties.

18.5. Issues and Remedies Related to NPAs

Economic Impact

- **Credit Crunch**: NPAs reduce available credit, affecting business expansion and employment.
- **Investment Slowdown**: High NPAs discourage investment, slowing economic growth.
- **Higher Interest Rates**: Banks may raise rates to compensate for NPA losses, impacting borrowers.
- **Systemic Risks**: High NPAs contribute to economic instability and potential crises.

Impact on Banking System

- **Capital and Profitability Erosion**: NPAs erode banks' capital and reduce profits.
- **Stress on Asset Quality**: Persistent NPAs deteriorate a bank's balance sheet, affecting depositor trust.

- **Operational Challenges**: Resources diverted for NPA management impact normal operations.
- **Loss of Trust**: High NPAs can reduce confidence among depositors and investors, impacting financial stability.

18.7. Remedies for NPAs: The Concept of a Bad Bank

A "bad bank" is a separate entity created to manage and recover NPAs. This solution enables banks to transfer troubled assets to the bad bank, isolating them from healthy assets, and focus on core banking activities.

Key Functions of a Bad Bank:

- **Asset Transfer**: Troubled assets move to a specialized entity focused on recovery.
- **Risk Isolation**: Separating NPAs allows banks to protect healthier assets and focus on core business.
- **Resolution and Recovery**: The bad bank, using expert teams, restructures or sells distressed assets.
- **Time-Bound Approach**: Aims for a quick resolution to minimize the adverse impact on the financial system.
- **Government Involvement**: Often backed by government support to manage systemic NPA issues.

The bad bank model, often linked with Asset Reconstruction Companies (ARCs), can streamline the handling of NPAs and contribute to improved financial stability.

UNIT III BANKING REFORMS AND REGULATORY CHANGES

Chapter 19 Narasimham Committee of Banking Reforms

Narasimham Committee Overview

The **Narasimham Committee**, also known as the **Committee on the Financial System**, was established by the Reserve Bank of India in **1991**, chaired by **M. Narasimham**, a former RBI governor. It aimed to reform and modernize India's financial system by addressing its **structure, organization, functions, and procedures**.

19.1. Narasimham Committee 1 (1991)

Objectives: The Committee aimed to:

- Review the Indian financial system.
- Recommend improvements in the banking sector.

Key Recommendations:

- **Introduction of Private Sector Banks:** Allowed private banks to operate, encouraging competition.
- **Deregulation of Interest Rates:** Suggested freeing interest rates from government control, promoting a market-based approach.
- **Strengthening Prudential Norms:** Urged the RBI to adopt stricter prudential norms to reduce risks.
- **Improved Bank Management:** Recommended professional management practices in banks.

- **New Regulatory Framework:** Proposed a robust regulatory structure for the financial sector.

Banking Sector Reforms:

- **Reduction of CRR and SLR:** Recommended lowering statutory pre-emptions like Cash Reserve Ratio (CRR) and Statutory Liquidity Ratio (SLR) to increase lendable funds.
- **Capital Adequacy:** Advocated for stronger capital adequacy norms for resilience.
- **Addressing NPAs:** Emphasized prudential norms to improve asset quality and reduce Non-Performing Assets (NPAs).
- **Technology Upgradation:** Stressed the need for modernization and adoption of technology in banking operations.
- **Financial Discipline and Autonomy:** Recommended enhancing the autonomy of RBI and suggested forming a **Board for Financial Supervision (BFS).**
- **Interest Rate Liberalization:** Proposed that interest rates be market-driven to enhance competitiveness.

Implementation: Many recommendations were implemented over the years, resulting in a more **competitive and efficient banking sector.**

19.2. Narasimham Committee 2 (1998)

The Narasimham Committee 2 focused on reviewing the reforms' progress and recommending further measures.

Key Recommendations:

- **Consolidation of Public Sector Banks:**
  - Suggested mergers and acquisitions to reduce the number of public sector banks.
- **New Capital Instruments:**
  - Advocated for banks to raise capital via instruments like **perpetual non-cumulative preference shares**.
- **Strengthening Corporate Governance:**
  - Emphasized improved corporate governance in banks.
- **Technology Adoption:**
  - Reinforced the importance of IT in improving operational efficiency.

Impact of Narasimham Committee Reforms:

- **Private Sector Entry:** Encouraged innovation and competition.
- **Interest Rate Deregulation:** Allowed banks to be more responsive to market conditions.
- **Stricter Prudential Norms:** Improved risk management and financial stability.
- **Bank Management:** Enhanced decision-making and efficiency in banks.

19.2.1. Challenges in the post-Narasimham Era

- **High NPAs:** Persistent NPAs due to corporate defaults.
- **Financial Inclusion:** Limited reach in rural areas, requiring greater outreach.
- **Technology Integration:** Rapid changes in technology necessitate constant updates.

- **Cybersecurity Threats:** Rising risks to digital banking systems.
- **Complex Regulatory Compliance:** Regulatory landscape is becoming increasingly challenging.

19.2.2. Opportunities in the Post-Reform Banking Sector

- **Growing Financial Services Market:** Expanding reach and product offerings due to rising incomes.
- **Financial Inclusion and Microfinance:** Serving underserved areas for inclusive growth.
- **Digital Banking and Fintech:** Leveraging technology to enhance services.
- **Rural Banking:** Expanding credit to rural and agricultural sectors.
- **Global Expansion:** Potential for Indian banks to explore international opportunities.

19.2.3 Criticism of Narasimham Committee Recommendations

- **Priority Sector Lending:** Concerns about reducing mandatory lending in sectors like agriculture.
- **Income Inequality:** Focus on profitability may overlook underserved communities.
- **Bank Employees:** Job security concerns due to cost-cutting measures.
- **Social Banking Impact:** Concerns over reduced focus on rural and underprivileged sectors.
- **Over-Emphasis on Deregulation:** Potential for excessive risk-taking in a deregulated environment.

- **Implementation Clarity:** Lack of clear guidelines for some recommendations.
- **Rural Banking Challenges:** Insufficient attention to rural banking needs.
- **Insensitivity to Local Contexts:** Standardized recommendations may not fit diverse regions.

19.2.4 Comparison with Other Reform Committees

- **Ghosh Committee (1979):**
  - Focused on public sector bank efficiency, cost control, and branch optimization.
- **Chakravarty Committee (1985):**
  - Recommended capital base strengthening, better customer service, and expanding financial inclusion.
- **MacMillan Committee (UK, 1962):**
  - Advocated competition in banking and innovation in products.
- **Hunt Commission (UK, 1979):**
  - Suggested removing restrictive regulations to promote competition.

Chapter 20 Changes in Banking Regulation

Changes in banking regulations refer to modifications, revisions, or updates made to the rules, policies, and guidelines that govern the operation and conduct of banks and other financial institutions within a specific jurisdiction. These changes are typically implemented by regulatory authorities, such as central banks or financial regulatory bodies, to address evolving economic conditions, financial stability concerns, technological advancements, and emerging risks in the banking industry. The primary objectives of banking regulations include safeguarding the interests of depositors, maintaining the stability of the financial system, and ensuring fair and transparent practices within the banking sector.

20.1. Key Aspects Subject to Changes in Banking Regulations

Changes in banking regulations often address several critical aspects within the banking sector. Some of these key aspects include:

- **Capital Adequacy Requirements:**
  - Regulations prescribe the minimum capital banks must maintain to absorb losses and ensure financial stability. Changes to these requirements are made to increase resilience and ensure banks are adequately capitalized.
- **Liquidity Standards:**
  - These regulations ensure banks have sufficient liquid assets to meet short-term obligations. Adjustments may be made to address liquidity risks and maintain financial system stability.

- **Risk Management Practices:**
  - Regulatory bodies may revise guidelines for managing risks like credit risk, operational risk, and market risk. These updates help improve the overall risk management framework within banks.
- **Consumer Protection:**
  - Changes are made to strengthen consumer protection, ensuring fair treatment of customers, transparency in banking operations, and the security of customer data.
- **Anti-Money Laundering (AML) and Counter-Terrorism Financing (CTF):**
  - Regulations in these areas are updated regularly to combat financial crimes. Changes may include stricter due diligence requirements and enhanced reporting obligations.
- **Digital Banking and Fintech:**
  - With the rise of digital banking and financial technologies (fintech), regulators may introduce new rules to accommodate technological advancements, ensure cybersecurity, and foster innovation while safeguarding consumer interests.
- **Resolution Mechanisms:**
  - Regulatory frameworks may be updated to improve the resolution of failing banks, ensuring that distressed institutions can be resolved efficiently without causing broader systemic disruptions.
- **Governance and Conduct Standards:**
  - Regulations set standards for bank governance, including board composition, risk management oversight, and ethical business practices. Changes aim to enhance accountability and transparency in banking operations.
- **Stress Testing Requirements:**

- ▪ Stress testing frameworks are often updated to reflect changing economic conditions and assess the resilience of banks under adverse scenarios.
- **Accounting Standards:**
  - ▪ Changes in accounting standards, such as IFRS (International Financial Reporting Standards) or GAAP (Generally Accepted Accounting Principles), can impact how banks report their financial positions and performance.
- **Basel III and Global Standards:**
  - ▪ Changes in domestic banking regulations may occur in response to international standards, like those from the Basel Committee on Banking Supervision, which influence global banking practices.

20.2. Reasons for Changes in Banking Regulations

Several factors drive the evolution of banking regulations:

- **New Technologies:**
  - ▪ The rise of digital banking, cryptocurrencies, and fintech innovations necessitates changes to ensure the financial system remains secure, efficient, and adaptable to these advancements.
- **Financial Crises:**
  - ▪ Financial crises, such as the 2008 global financial meltdown, often lead to the introduction of stricter regulations to prevent similar crises in the future and to enhance stability within the financial sector.
- **Global Coordination:**
  - ▪ International agreements, such as those by the Basel Committee, often lead to regulatory changes to

ensure a level playing field for banks across borders, harmonizing regulations globally.

- **Consumer Protection:**
  - The rise of cybercrime and other emerging threats has prompted regulatory updates focused on protecting consumers, ensuring fair treatment, and securing sensitive financial data.

20.3. Challenges and Needs in Banking Regulations

While changes in banking regulations are necessary to adapt to new challenges, there are several issues regulators must navigate:

- **Finding the Right Balance:**
  - Regulations need to be strict enough to prevent risks (such as financial instability or fraud) but not so restrictive that they stifle innovation or economic growth within the banking sector.
- **Keeping Up with the Pace of Change:**
  - The rapid evolution of financial technologies, market conditions, and global economic shifts requires regulations that can adapt swiftly to these changes.
- **International Cooperation:**
  - Different countries may have varying regulatory frameworks, making it challenging to create unified global standards, particularly in cross-border banking and financial transactions.
- **Enforcing Regulations:**
  - Effective enforcement mechanisms are crucial to ensuring compliance by banks with the updated regulations. This is essential to maintain the integrity of the financial system.

20.4. Objectives and Limitations of Banking Regulations

Objectives:

- **Maintaining Financial Stability:**
    - Preventing bank failures and ensuring the overall stability of the financial system.
- **Protecting Consumers:**
    - Ensuring fair treatment of customers and protecting their deposits and investments from financial instability or mismanagement.
- **Promoting Competition:**
    - Encouraging a level playing field for all banks and financial institutions, fostering innovation, and improving service offerings.
- **Combating Financial Crime:**
    - Preventing illegal activities like money laundering, terrorism financing, and fraud.

Limitations:

- **Complexity:**
    - Regulations can be complex, making them difficult to understand and navigate even for financial professionals, leading to potential compliance challenges.
- **Costs:**
    - The implementation and compliance with regulations can incur significant costs for banks, which may eventually be passed on to consumers through higher fees or reduced services.

- **Unintended Consequences:**
  - New regulations may inadvertently stifle innovation, create new loopholes, or lead to unintended negative consequences that require further regulatory changes.

20.5. Recent Changes in Banking Regulations in India

Union Budget 2023-24:

- **Proposed Amendments to Key Acts:**
  - The Union Budget proposed amendments to key banking-related laws like the **Banking Regulation Act**, **Banking Companies Act**, and **Reserve Bank of India Act**. These amendments aim to:
    - Improve **bank governance**.
    - Enhance **investor protection**.
    - Facilitate **strategic disinvestments** in public sector banks.
- **Increased Deposit Limits for Senior Citizens:**
  - The maximum deposit limits for schemes like **Senior Citizen Savings Scheme** and **Monthly Income Account Scheme** have been doubled, benefiting elderly individuals by providing more favourable investment options.
- **Centralized Data Processing for Companies:**
  - A **centralized platform** is proposed for handling company filings under the **Companies Act**, aiming to expedite processes and improve the ease of doing business in India.

- **Integrated IT Portal for Unclaimed Shares and Dividends:**
  - A new integrated portal under the **Investor Education and Protection Fund Authority** will simplify the process of reclaiming unclaimed shares and dividends, enhancing transparency and accessibility.

20.6. Other Recent Changes in Banking Regulations:

- **Draft Cryptocurrency and Regulation of Official Digital Currency Bill, 2021:**
  - This bill aims to create a framework for an **official digital currency** by the Reserve Bank of India (RBI) and may ban **private cryptocurrencies**. It reflects efforts to regulate digital currencies and safeguard the Indian financial system from associated risks.
- **Payment and Settlement Systems Act (Amendment) Bill, 2023:**
  - This bill strengthens the **RBI's regulatory powers** over payment systems and aims to prevent fraud, enhancing the security and efficiency of digital payment systems in India.
- **Mahila Samman Savings Certificate (2023):**
  - Introduced in February 2023, this scheme offers attractive interest rates for deposits made by **women and girls**, promoting **financial inclusion** and providing women with better access to secure and profitable investment opportunities.

The ongoing evolution of banking regulations plays a critical role in maintaining financial stability, promoting innovation, and protecting consumers. In India, recent changes focus on improving governance, enhancing investor protection, and addressing emerging financial risks, such as those posed by digital currencies and fintech innovations. Balancing the objectives of stability, innovation, and consumer protection while navigating challenges such as complexity and enforcement remains an ongoing task for regulators.

Chapter 21 Deregulation of Interest Rate

The deregulation of interest rates in India marks a significant transition in the country's banking sector, moving from a system of government-imposed controls to one where interest rates are determined by market forces. This process has aimed to liberalize the financial sector, increase efficiency, and improve the transmission of monetary policy. Below is a detailed exploration of the process, benefits, challenges, and ongoing developments related to interest rate deregulation in India.

21.1. Process of Deregulation:

The transition from regulated interest rates to a deregulated system has been gradual, with key milestones implemented over the years to move toward market-driven pricing:

- **Introduction of Base Rate (2010):** The RBI introduced the Base Rate system in 2010, replacing the earlier Benchmark Prime Lending Rate (BPLR). The Base Rate was designed to reflect the true cost of funds for banks, thereby increasing transparency and ensuring that the rates banks charged borrowers were based on their actual cost of funds.
- **Marginal Cost of Funds-Based Lending Rate (MCLR) (2016):** In 2016, the RBI introduced the MCLR system, which considers various factors such as the marginal cost of funds, the negative carry of the Cash Reserve Ratio (CRR), operating costs, and tenor premium. The MCLR framework was designed to be more dynamic and reflective of actual market conditions compared to the Base Rate system.
- **Linking Retail Loans to External Benchmarks (2019):** In 2019, the RBI mandated that new floating-rate loans, particularly retail loans and small business loans, be linked

to an external benchmark. This was intended to enhance the transmission of monetary policy changes to lending rates. The external benchmarks included rates like the RBI's repo rate, government securities yield, or any other benchmark that the banks might choose.

- **Repo Rate-Linked Lending Rates (RLLR):** Several banks have also adopted the Repo Rate-Linked Lending Rates (RLLR) system, wherein lending rates are directly tied to the RBI's repo rate. This ensures that fluctuations in the repo rate result in automatic adjustments in the interest rates charged on loans, making it easier for borrowers to gauge changes in their monthly payments in response to RBI monetary policy actions.

21.2. Impact and Benefits:

The deregulation of interest rates in India has led to several positive changes in the banking sector:

- **Market-driven Interest Rates:** Banks now have the flexibility to set their interest rates based on the cost of funds, market conditions, and competition. This has led to a more competitive banking environment, where banks must attract customers by offering competitive rates.
- **Improved Transmission of Monetary Policy:** With the move to linking loans to external benchmarks, such as the repo rate, there is a more direct link between the RBI's monetary policy actions and the rates charged to borrowers. This helps to ensure that changes in the policy rate are more efficiently transmitted to the end customer, which can influence borrowing and investment decisions.
- **Enhanced Transparency:** The introduction of the Base Rate, MCLR, and external benchmarks has improved

transparency in how banks determine interest rates. Customers can better understand how their loan rates are set, making it easier for them to compare rates across different banks.

- **Flexibility for Banks:** Deregulation allows banks to adjust interest rates based on their individual cost of funds and market conditions, providing them with greater flexibility in managing their business operations and profit margins.

21.3. Challenges:

Despite its benefits, interest rate deregulation also presents several challenges for banks and borrowers:

- **Interest Rate Risk:** Banks now face greater interest rate risk because their profitability is directly influenced by market fluctuations. For example, if interest rates increase, banks might experience higher borrowing costs, which can negatively affect their margins unless they adjust their lending rates accordingly.
- **Transmission Challenges:** While linking loans to external benchmarks was intended to improve the transmission of monetary policy, there have been instances where the reduction in RBI policy rates has not been fully passed on to borrowers. This can create a disconnect between the central bank's actions and the interest rates faced by customers.
- **Impact on Margins:** With deregulated interest rates, banks need to manage their net interest margins (the difference between the interest earned on loans and the interest paid on deposits) carefully. As market rates become more volatile, banks face the challenge of adjusting their asset-liability positions dynamically.

21.4. Ongoing Developments:

Interest rate deregulation is an ongoing process, and the RBI continues to refine its approach to improve the effectiveness of this framework. Some of the ongoing developments include:

- **Monitoring and Adjusting Frameworks:** The RBI regularly reviews the MCLR and external benchmark frameworks to ensure that they are working efficiently and transparently. Any necessary changes or adjustments are made to improve the alignment between the market and the policy goals.
- **Increased Focus on Consumer Protection:** While deregulation enhances competition, the RBI also ensures that consumers are protected from unfair practices. There is a continuous focus on improving transparency and preventing any mispricing of risk.
- **Alignment with Global Standards:** The RBI's policies on interest rate deregulation are also in line with global best practices, ensuring that India's banking system remains competitive and resilient to international financial shifts.

The deregulation of interest rates in India has brought about significant improvements in market efficiency, transparency, and monetary policy transmission. While challenges like interest rate risk and transmission gaps remain, the system has offered banks more flexibility in their operations and has helped foster a more competitive and transparent financial environment. Moving forward, the RBI will likely continue to adapt and refine its policies to address emerging challenges and enhance the functioning of the banking sector. For the most up-to-date information on this subject, it is advisable to refer to the latest guidelines issued by the Reserve Bank of India.

Chapter 22 Capital Adequacy and BASEL Norms

The **Capital Adequacy Ratio (CAR)**, also known as the **Capital to Risk (Weighted) Assets Ratio (CRAR)**, is a critical measure of a bank's financial health. It represents the ratio of a bank's capital to its risk-weighted assets and current liabilities. This ratio helps ensure that banks have enough capital to absorb potential losses from credit risk, operational risk, and market risk, thereby securing depositors and enhancing the stability of the financial system. Below is an explanation of the components, regulatory requirements, and global standards related to CAR.

22.1. Capital Adequacy:

Capital adequacy refers to the sufficiency of a bank's capital in relation to the risks it faces. It ensures that a bank has enough financial resources to cover potential losses and remain solvent during adverse economic conditions. The primary objectives of capital adequacy are:

- **Protecting depositors:** Adequate capital safeguards the funds of depositors and prevents the bank from becoming insolvent.
- **Maintaining financial system stability:** Sufficient capital helps to maintain the stability of the broader financial system by reducing the risk of systemic failure.
- **Boosting market confidence:** A strong capital base enhances public trust in the bank's ability to withstand financial shocks and risks.

In essence, the Capital Adequacy Ratio (CAR) helps determine whether a bank is operating with enough capital to absorb unexpected losses and continue its operations smoothly.

22.2. Components of Capital:

The capital base of a bank is divided into two primary components: **Tier 1 Capital** and **Tier 2 Capital**. Each component plays a distinct role in ensuring the financial strength and stability of the bank.

- **Tier 1 Capital:** Often referred to as the core capital, Tier 1 capital consists of high-quality, stable capital that can easily absorb losses. This includes:
  - **Common Equity:** The primary source of capital that includes common stock, retained earnings, and other reserves.
  - **Retained Earnings:** Profits that are not distributed as dividends but are kept within the bank to build capital reserves.

    Tier 1 capital is the most secure form of capital because it can absorb losses in times of financial stress.

- **Tier 2 Capital:** This includes supplementary capital that can be used to absorb losses but is considered less secure compared to Tier 1. Tier 2 capital may consist of:
  - **Subordinated Debt:** Debt that ranks below other forms of debt in the case of liquidation.
  - **Hybrid Instruments:** A combination of debt and equity, such as convertible bonds.
  - **Other Less Secure Financing:** Other sources of capital that are less permanent but can still contribute to the bank's financial strength.

22.3. Regulatory Requirements:

Regulators establish minimum capital requirements that banks must maintain to ensure financial stability and protect depositors. These requirements are typically expressed as a percentage of risk-weighted assets (RWA), which accounts for the different levels of risk associated with various asset classes held by the bank.

- **Risk-Weighted Assets (RWA):** RWA considers the credit risk, market risk, and operational risk associated with different assets. The riskier an asset, the higher the weight assigned to it when calculating RWA.

Basel Norms:

The **Basel Committee on Banking Supervision** developed a series of international banking regulations known as the **Basel Accords** (or Basel Norms) to standardize capital adequacy requirements globally. These regulations aim to strengthen the banking sector and promote financial stability. The most notable Basel accords are **Basel I**, **Basel II**, and **Basel III**.

Basel I (1988):

- Basel I was the first major international attempt to address capital adequacy, focusing primarily on **credit risk**.
- It introduced a **minimum capital requirement** of 8% of a bank's total risk-weighted assets, with the primary goal of ensuring that banks had sufficient capital to cover potential credit losses.

Basel II (2004):

- Basel II provided a more **risk-sensitive** approach to capital adequacy, considering not only credit risk but also **operational** and **market risks**.
- It introduced the concept of **internal risk assessment models** for banks to determine their capital requirements based on their own risk exposures.
- Basel II emphasized the need for **supervisory review** and **market discipline** to assess a bank's risk profile.

Basel III (2010):

- Basel III was introduced in response to the **2007-2008 financial crisis** and aimed to address shortcomings in the banking system that were exposed during the crisis.
- Basel III introduced more **stringent capital requirements** and enhanced the **quality** of capital by focusing on **common equity**.
- It also introduced the **capital conservation buffer**, which requires banks to build up capital during times of economic growth to withstand economic downturns.
- Basel III introduced additional standards related to **liquidity** and **leverage ratios**, designed to strengthen banks' ability to withstand financial stress and reduce systemic risk.

22.4. Key Principles of Basel III:

Basel III introduced several key principles to ensure banks maintain robust capital buffers and liquidity standards:

- **Minimum Capital Requirements:** Basel III raised the minimum capital ratios, particularly the **common equity**

tier 1 (CET1) capital, which must be at least 4.5% of risk-weighted assets, with a total capital ratio of at least 8%.

- **Capital Conservation Buffer:** Banks must hold an additional **2.5%** of capital over the minimum requirement, effectively increasing the total capital ratio to 10.5% during periods of economic stability.
- **Leverage Ratio:** Basel III introduced a **leverage ratio**, which limits the amount of leverage banks can take on by restricting the ratio of the bank's capital to its total assets.
- **Liquidity Coverage Ratio (LCR):** This ratio requires banks to maintain sufficient high-quality liquid assets (HQLAs) to cover net cash outflows for a 30-day period under stressed conditions.
- **Net Stable Funding Ratio (NSFR):** The NSFR aims to encourage banks to maintain a stable funding profile over the longer term by comparing the bank's available stable funding to its required stable funding.

22.5. Global Adoption:

The **Basel norms** have been widely adopted by countries around the world, influencing national regulatory frameworks and promoting consistency in global banking regulation. The implementation of Basel III, however, varies by country, with regulators adapting the norms to their own domestic conditions and economic environments.

The **Capital Adequacy Ratio (CAR)** is a key measure of a bank's financial health, determining whether it has sufficient capital to cover its risks. The regulatory frameworks of the **Basel Accords**, particularly **Basel III**, have significantly enhanced global banking standards, improved the resilience of banks, and reduced the risk of systemic failure. As banking systems continue to evolve, maintaining robust capital adequacy is crucial for ensuring the stability of financial institutions and the broader financial system.

Chapter 23 Governance Issues

The **Capital Adequacy Ratio (CAR)** and **Basel norms** are designed to strengthen the financial stability of banks, ensuring they have sufficient capital to absorb losses and manage risk. However, there are several **governance issues** that can arise in the implementation of these regulatory frameworks. These issues can affect their effectiveness, leading to challenges in maintaining the stability and resilience of the banking sector. Below are some of the key governance concerns related to capital adequacy and Basel norms:

Inconsistent Implementation Across Jurisdictions: The **Basel norms** are internationally recognized, but their implementation can vary significantly across different countries and jurisdictions. While Basel III aims for global regulatory consistency, individual countries may adapt the norms to suit their domestic financial environments. This can create **regulatory arbitrage**, were banks exploit differences in regulations between jurisdictions, leading to potential weaknesses in the global banking system. Globally active banks might also face complexities in complying with diverse regulations across borders, undermining the spirit of the Basel accords.

Regulatory Capture: It occurs when the institutions being regulated exert undue influence on the regulatory authorities. In such cases, regulators may adopt rules and standards that align more closely with the interests of the financial institutions they oversee, rather than serving the broader public interest. This can lead to **weaker regulatory standards**, compromising the stability of the banking sector and potentially creating opportunities for risk-taking behaviors that harm the economy.

Lack of Timely Updates: Financial markets and banking institutions are dynamic, constantly evolving in response to new risks, innovations, and global economic changes. However, **delays in updating Basel norms** can result in regulations that are not well-equipped to address emerging risks. For example, the rise of fintech, cryptocurrency, and other technological innovations may pose new risks that were not adequately addressed in earlier versions of the Basel framework. The failure to adapt regulations promptly could leave banks exposed to unanticipated challenges.

Complexity of Basel Frameworks: The **Basel II and Basel III** frameworks are intricate, involving complex calculations, risk assessments, and requirements for different types of capital. While these frameworks are designed to be risk-sensitive, their complexity can create challenges for both **regulators and financial institutions** in terms of understanding, implementing, and complying with the regulations. This complexity might lead to misinterpretations, operational inefficiencies, and errors in capital requirements or risk management practices.

Risk Model Reliance: Basel II introduced the concept of using internal **risk models** developed by individual banks to assess their capital requirements. While this allows banks to adopt a more tailored approach to their risk profiles, over-reliance on these models without proper oversight can lead to **inaccurate risk assessments**. If a bank's risk models are poorly designed or manipulated to lower capital requirements, it could result in the bank being undercapitalized and unable to absorb losses during periods of financial stress.

Procyclicality: One of the criticisms of the **Basel III framework** is that it can be **procyclical**, meaning that it may exacerbate economic cycles rather than mitigate them. For instance, during an economic downturn, Basel III requires banks to hold more capital, which could restrict their ability to lend. This could **amplify the recessionary pressures** by reducing the availability of credit in the economy. Conversely, during times of economic growth, when capital requirements are more easily met, banks may increase their lending, potentially inflating asset bubbles.

Compliance Challenges for Smaller Institutions: Smaller banks often face greater challenges in complying with the complex Basel frameworks due to limited resources and expertise. Implementing the necessary risk models, systems, and controls to meet the regulatory requirements can be costly and time-consuming for smaller institutions. This could place them at a disadvantage compared to larger banks with more resources, leading to **regulatory arbitrage** and potentially undermining the competitiveness of smaller players in the market.

Unintended Consequences: Changes in capital adequacy requirements or other regulatory measures can have unintended side effects. For example, banks may adjust their business models to meet the new capital requirements by focusing more on **low-risk assets** or **short-term lending**, potentially exposing them to different types of risks. These unintended consequences may pose new challenges to the financial system, such as the creation of **new forms of risk** or the concentration of risk in certain sectors.

Measurement of Risk: Accurate risk measurement is crucial for determining the appropriate capital requirements. However, governance issues can arise when there are challenges in consistently and reliably measuring risks. If banks or regulators fail to adopt accurate, timely, and transparent methods for assessing risks such as credit, operational, and market risks, the **capital levels** set may be misaligned with the actual risks faced by the institution. This can result in **insufficient capital buffers** and heightened exposure to potential losses.

Inadequate Supervision and Enforcement: Even with strong regulatory frameworks in place, **weak supervision and enforcement** can undermine their effectiveness. If regulatory authorities fail to properly monitor banks' adherence to capital adequacy requirements or do not take appropriate actions against non-compliant institutions, banks may take excessive risks without adequate capital reserves. This lack of **accountability** could lead to **systemic risks** and instability in the financial system.

Insufficient Public Disclosure: Transparency is essential for maintaining **market discipline** and ensuring investor confidence in the financial system. If banks fail to disclose key information about their **capital adequacy**, **risk profile**, or **compliance with Basel norms**, it becomes more difficult for investors, analysts, and the public to assess the health of individual institutions. **Lack of public disclosure** could lead to reduced market confidence and **investor uncertainty**, increasing the risk of financial instability.

While the **Capital Adequacy Ratio (CAR)** and **Basel norms** are pivotal for ensuring the stability and resilience of banks, there are several **governance issues** that could undermine their effectiveness. These issues, such as **inconsistent implementation**, **regulatory capture**, **complexity**, and **procyclicality**, can create challenges for both regulators and financial institutions. Addressing these governance concerns is critical to ensure that capital adequacy regulations continue to fulfil their primary objective of safeguarding financial stability and protecting depositors in an increasingly complex and interconnected global financial system.

UNIT IV EXPLORING INSURANCE

Chapter 24 Insurance – Basic Issues

Insurance is a financial mechanism designed to provide protection or reimbursement against specified risks or losses by transferring the financial burden from an individual or entity (the **policyholder**) to an insurance company (the **insurer**). The policyholder pays periodic payments known as **premiums** to the insurer, who, in turn, offers coverage as outlined in a **policy** — a contractual agreement that defines the terms, conditions, coverage, and exclusions of the insurance.

24.1 Key Components of Insurance:

- **Policyholder**: The person or entity purchasing the insurance policy, seeking financial protection.
- **Insurance Company (Insurer)**: The organization that provides insurance coverage and assumes the financial risks associated with the policy.
- **Premium**: The periodic payment made by the policyholder to the insurer to maintain the insurance coverage.
- **Policy**: The written agreement that defines the scope of coverage, terms, exclusions, and other conditions.

24.2 Types of Insurance:

There are several different types of insurance, each designed to cover specific risks:

- **Life Insurance**: Offers financial protection to the beneficiaries in the event of the policyholder's death. Some life insurance policies also include investment components, making them a hybrid of insurance and investment.

- **Health Insurance**: Covers medical expenses, such as hospitalization, surgeries, preventive care, and prescription drugs.
- **Property Insurance**: Protects physical property (e.g., homes, cars, and businesses) against damage or loss, with specific types like homeowners' and auto insurance.
- **Liability Insurance**: Covers the policyholder's legal responsibility for injuries or damage caused to others.
- **Business Insurance**: Provides protection against risks faced by businesses, including property damage, liability, and business interruption.
- **Auto Insurance**: Offers coverage for vehicles against damages, theft, and accidents.
- **Travel Insurance**: Protects against unexpected events while traveling, such as trip cancellations, medical emergencies, or lost baggage.

24.3 Importance of Insurance:

Insurance plays a critical role in managing risk and ensuring financial security:

- **Risk Mitigation**: Allows the policyholder to transfer financial risk to the insurer, making unexpected losses more manageable.
- **Financial Security**: Provides financial protection against risks such as accidents, illnesses, or property damage.
- **Promotes Economic Stability**: By spreading risk across a large pool of policyholders, insurance helps stabilize economies, especially in times of crisis.
- **Encourages Savings**: Certain insurance types, like life insurance, also function as savings or investment vehicles, promoting financial discipline.

24.4 Objectives of Insurance:

The core objectives of insurance can be broken down into four key goals:

- **Risk Transfer**: Insurance allows individuals and businesses to transfer the financial burden of potential losses to the insurer.
- **Financial Protection**: It offers a safety net, providing monetary support to policyholders when they face unforeseen financial burdens.
- **Promoting Stability**: By pooling risk, insurance helps to prevent individual financial crises from becoming systemic issues.
- **Encouraging Prudent Behavior**: Some types of insurance, such as auto insurance or health insurance, encourage policyholders to take risk-reducing actions to lower their premiums.

24.5 Limitations of Insurance:

While insurance provides significant benefits, there are some notable limitations:

- **Premium Costs**: The cost of premiums may be a barrier, especially for individuals or businesses with limited financial resources.
- **Exclusions and Limitations**: Insurance policies often have exclusions or limitations that prevent coverage for certain risks, leaving gaps in protection.
- **Moral Hazard**: The presence of insurance might encourage risky behavior, knowing that financial losses will be covered by the insurer.

- **Claim Processing Delays**: Sometimes, the process of filing and receiving claims can be slow or complicated, causing frustration for policyholders.
- **Complexity of Policies**: Understanding insurance terms, conditions, and coverage details can be challenging, especially for people with limited financial literacy.

24.6 Challenges in the Insurance Industry:

The insurance industry faces several hurdles, some of which are related to global trends and technological changes:

- **Technological Disruption**: The integration of new technologies like artificial intelligence (AI) and big data presents both opportunities (e.g., more accurate risk assessment) and challenges (e.g., cybersecurity risks, data privacy).
- **Regulatory Compliance**: Insurance companies must navigate complex and constantly evolving regulations that vary by jurisdiction, creating compliance burdens.
- **Cybersecurity Risks**: As insurers increasingly rely on digital platforms, they face the risk of cyberattacks, which could expose sensitive customer data.
- **Climate Change and Natural Disasters**: The increasing frequency and severity of natural disasters challenge insurers to assess and manage risks effectively, often leading to higher premiums or restricted coverage.
- **Changing Demographics**: An aging population may lead to greater demand for health and life insurance, presenting challenges related to risk management and pricing.
- **Globalization**: Insurers operating across multiple regions face difficulties in adapting to varying regulations and market conditions in each jurisdiction.

- **Competition**: The highly competitive nature of the insurance market means that companies must innovate to attract and retain customers, often leading to price wars or new product offerings.
- **Fraud**: Fraudulent claims pose a persistent challenge, with insurers needing to implement effective fraud detection and prevention mechanisms.

Insurance, despite its crucial role in providing financial security and mitigating risk, remains a complex industry to understand and navigate. The learner must comprehend its key components, types, and the limitations and challenges that the industry faces. It's not merely about memorizing terms, but understanding how the system operates and why it's difficult to manage, especially in a rapidly changing world marked by new risks, technologies, and regulations.

Chapter 25 Risk Pooling and Risk Transfer

Risk pooling and risk transfer are fundamental concepts in the concepts of **Risk Pooling** and **Risk Transfer** from the foundational principles of how insurance functions. These concepts are essential for the insurance industry to provide financial protection against unforeseen events by spreading and transferring risks across large groups of policyholders.

25.1 Risk Pooling:

Risk pooling refers to the practice of combining individual risks into a larger, diversified group or pool. This enables the spreading of financial risks across many people or entities, reducing the financial burden on any single member. The idea is that, within the group, not all policyholders will experience losses at the same time, which ensures that the collective risk is manageable.

- **Diversification**: By pooling risks from a variety of sources, insurers benefit from the **law of large numbers**. This principle suggests that as the number of participants increases, the overall risk becomes more predictable. With a larger pool, unexpected losses are less likely to have a significant impact.
- **Predictability**: While individual losses are unpredictable, the overall loss for the entire group becomes easier to forecast. This allows insurers to calculate more accurate premium rates.
- **Financial Stability**: Risk pooling helps stabilize the financial burden of any individual loss. The financial impact of a loss is shared across the pool, ensuring that the cost is distributed and reducing the strain on any one person.

- **Social Benefit**: On a societal level, risk pooling prevents financial hardship for those who would struggle to recover from significant losses on their own. By contributing to the pool, members protect each other from extreme financial events.

25.2 Risk Transfer:

Risk transfer refers to the process by which an individual or business shifts the financial consequences of potential losses to an insurer. When a person purchases insurance, they effectively transfer the risk of certain events (e.g., accidents, illness, or property damage) to the insurance company.

- **Contractual Agreement**: An insurance policy is a formal contract that defines the terms under which the insurer will take on the policyholder's risk. In exchange for the payment of premiums, the insurer agrees to cover certain types of loss or damage.
- **Financial Responsibility**: Upon the occurrence of a covered event, the insurer becomes responsible for providing financial compensation, as stipulated in the insurance contract. This shifts the financial risk away from the policyholder.
- **Premiums as Consideration**: The premium paid by the policyholder serves as the consideration or payment for the risk transfer. Essentially, the policyholder is paying the insurer to take on the risk associated with certain events.
- **Limits and Deductibles**: Insurance policies often specify limits (maximum amounts the insurer will pay) and deductibles (the portion of the loss the policyholder must pay before insurance kicks in). These elements define the extent of the risk transfer.

- **Legal and Financial Protection**: Risk transfer provides legal and financial protection, ensuring that the policyholder is shielded from the financial consequences of certain risks. This protection gives individuals and businesses peace of mind.

25.3 Relationship Between Risk Pooling and Risk Transfer:

Risk pooling and risk transfer are deeply interconnected, working together to create a robust insurance system.

- **Complementary Concepts**: While risk pooling focuses on collecting and spreading risks across a large group, risk transfer shifts the burden of those risks from the individual to the insurer. They work in tandem, as pooling makes it possible for insurers to take on the risk transferred by policyholders.
- **Risk Pooling Enables Risk Transfer**: By pooling a large number of risks, insurers can better assess the overall risk exposure and establish fair premiums. This creates the financial stability necessary to make risk transfer viable. A large, diversified pool makes it possible for the insurer to cover individual losses without overwhelming its resources.
- **Collective Financial Security**: Both risk pooling and risk transfer contribute to the overall financial security of the insured group. Risk pooling ensures that the group is financially stable, while risk transfer provides individual policyholders with protection from large, unforeseen expenses.

Risk Pooling and **Risk Transfer** are critical to how insurance works. **Risk Pooling** allows insurers to aggregate a large and diverse group of risks, making it easier to predict and manage financial losses. **Risk Transfer** allows policyholders to shift the financial burden of specific risks to insurers in exchange for premiums. Together, these concepts help provide financial security to individuals and businesses, enabling them to recover from unexpected events without facing debilitating financial hardship.

Chapter 26 Economic and Legal Perspective in Insurance

26.1 Economic Perspectives in Insurance

Insurance is a key element of the modern economic system, providing financial protection to individuals, businesses, and societies against various risks. It involves the distribution of financial uncertainty across a pool of participants, with the aim of stabilizing the economic environment. The economic principles of risk, market mechanisms, legal systems, and the evolution of technologies like Insurtech all contribute to the functioning and development of the insurance industry. Below is an exploration of the economic facets of insurance.

26.2 Fundamental Economic Concepts in Insurance:

- **Risk and Uncertainty:** Insurance deals primarily with risk and uncertainty. Risk refers to situations where the possibility of loss exists, while uncertainty pertains to situations where outcomes are indeterminate. Insurance works by spreading risk across many individuals, which reduces the financial burden for any single participant when a loss occurs.

- **Time Value of Money:** The time value of money is crucial in insurance because premiums paid today are invested and used to cover future claims. The value of money changes over time due to factors like inflation, interest rates, and the opportunity cost of capital. Insurers consider this principle when pricing premiums, assessing claims, and making financial projections.

- **Utility and Risk Aversion:** Individuals and businesses generally seek to maximize their utility, which is a measure of satisfaction or value derived from economic choices.

Most individuals are risk-averse, preferring certainty to uncertainty. Insurance helps mitigate the effects of risk aversion by providing financial protection against uncertain future events, thereby increasing economic utility for policyholders.

26.3 Market Dynamics in Insurance:

- **Supply and Demand in Insurance Markets:** Insurance markets operate on the principles of supply and demand. Insurers supply a range of insurance products to meet the demand from individuals and businesses seeking protection against risks. The balance between supply and demand, influenced by factors such as risk profiles, competition, and regulatory conditions, helps determine premium rates.

- **Adverse Selection and Moral Hazard:** Adverse selection occurs when individuals with higher risks are more likely to purchase insurance, leading to an imbalanced risk pool. Moral hazard arises when individuals or businesses take greater risks because they are protected by insurance. Both issues are managed by insurers through underwriting (evaluating risk profiles) and loss control measures.

- **Market Structure: Competition and Monopoly** The structure of the insurance market affects efficiency, pricing, and consumer choices. Competitive markets typically encourage innovation and lower prices, whereas monopolies can restrict options and drive-up costs. Many regulatory regimes aim to balance the benefits of competition with the need for stability in the insurance industry.

26.4 Regulatory Considerations:

- **Prudential Regulation:** Prudential regulation ensures that insurers remain financially solvent and able to meet future claims. Regulators require insurance companies to maintain sufficient capital reserves and conduct stress tests to assess their ability to withstand economic shocks. These regulations are essential for maintaining the stability of the insurance industry and protecting policyholders.

- **Consumer Protection:** Consumer protection regulations are critical in ensuring that insurance companies treat policyholders fairly. These include requirements for transparency in policy terms, fair marketing practices, and the establishment of processes for resolving disputes. Regulations also mandate that insurers act in good faith when handling claims.

- **Market Conduct Regulation:** Market conduct regulations govern the behavior of insurance companies, brokers, and agents to prevent fraud, deception, and unfair practices. These regulations help ensure that consumers are treated ethically and that the insurance marketplace remains trustworthy and efficient.

26.5 Economic Impact of Insurance:

- **Risk Management and Economic Stability:** Insurance plays a crucial role in maintaining economic stability by allowing risks to be shared and managed. By spreading the financial burden of unforeseen events, insurance reduces the overall economic impact of such events on individuals, businesses, and the economy as a whole. This contributes to maintaining investor confidence and fostering economic growth.

- **Resilience to Catastrophic Events:** Insurance provides a financial safety net that helps society recover from catastrophic events like natural disasters or pandemics. By pooling and transferring risks, insurance companies allow businesses and individuals to recover faster, reducing the economic impact and promoting societal resilience.

- **Capital Markets and Insurance-Linked Securities (ILS):** Insurance companies are increasingly using capital markets to manage risk through innovative financial instruments like insurance-linked securities (ILS). These instruments, such as catastrophe bonds, allow investors to participate in the risk management process, providing insurers with additional capital while offering investors diversification opportunities.

26.6 Legal Perspectives in Insurance:

- **Insurance Contract:** An insurance contract is a legally binding agreement between the insurer and the policyholder. For the contract to be valid, it must meet basic legal requirements: offer, acceptance, consideration (the premium), legal capacity, and a legal purpose. The terms of the contract, including coverage limits, exclusions, and premiums, must be adhered to by both parties.

- **Regulation and Compliance:** Insurance is heavily regulated by governmental bodies to ensure financial stability, protect consumers, and promote fair practices. Insurance companies must adhere to licensing requirements, and regulatory bodies enforce rules about transparency, pricing, and claims handling. Consumers are also protected through laws that govern disclosure, policy terms, and the claims process.

- **Policyholder Rights and Obligations:** Policyholders have the right to clear information about their policies, including coverage, exclusions, and claims processes. Insurers are required to act fairly and process claims promptly. Policyholders also have obligations to provide accurate information during the underwriting process and to fulfil the terms of their insurance contract.

- **Insurance Litigation:** Disputes can arise in insurance, particularly around issues of coverage. Courts may interpret policy language to determine whether a claim is valid. Insurance litigation can also involve "bad faith" claims, where insurers deny claims unfairly or delay payments. Insurance fraud is another significant issue, with legal actions taken against policyholders who provide false information or attempt fraudulent activities.

- **Reinsurance:** Reinsurance is the practice where insurers transfer a portion of their risks to other insurers. Reinsurance contracts are legally binding and specify the terms under which risk is shared between parties. Disputes in reinsurance may be settled through arbitration or mediation, depending on the contract terms.

- **Emerging Legal Issues:** As the insurance industry evolves, new legal challenges emerge, especially in areas like cyber insurance and climate-related risks. Legal issues related to data protection, privacy laws, and the potential liability of insurers for failing to adequately cover climate-related risks are increasingly relevant as the industry adapts to changing global circumstances.

Chapter 27 Social Vs Private Insurance

Social insurance and private insurance are two distinct models of providing financial protection against risks, and they differ in terms of their objectives, sources of funding, and the scope of coverage. Let's explore the key differences between social insurance and private insurance:

SL.No.	Basis of difference	Social Insurance	Private Insurance
1	Objective	The primary goal of social insurance is to promote social welfare and provide a safety net for the entire population. It aims to address social and economic inequalities by ensuring that everyone has access to essential services and financial support during times of need.	Risk Management for Individuals: Private insurance is designed to meet the individual risk management needs of policyholders. It aims to protect individuals or businesses against specific risks, and the coverage is tailored to the preferences and needs of the insured.
2	Funding	Public Contributions: Social insurance is typically funded through mandatory contributions	Individual Premiums: Private insurance is funded through individual premiums paid by policyholders. The

		from the public. These contributions may take the form of payroll taxes or other compulsory payments. The funding is often managed by a government agency.	cost of coverage is based on factors such as risk profile, coverage limits, and deductibles.
3	**Scope of Coverage**	Universal or Targeted: Social insurance programs are often designed to provide coverage to entire populations or specific groups, such as the elderly, disabled, or unemployed. Coverage is often universal, ensuring that everyone is included, regardless of individual risk profiles.	Selective and Customized: Private insurance allows individuals to choose coverage based on their specific needs. Policies can be highly customizable, and individuals can opt for coverage that aligns with their unique risk exposures.
4	**Example**	Social Security: Government-operated programs, such as Social	Life Insurance: Provides financial protection to beneficiaries in the event of the

		Security in the United States or similar schemes in other countries, provide financial support to retirees, disabled individuals, and survivors. Unemployment Insurance: Programs that offer financial assistance to individuals who lose their jobs. National Health Insurance: Systems that provide healthcare coverage to all citizens, funded through public contributions.	policyholder's death. Property and Casualty Insurance: Covers damages to property, liability for injuries, and other risks associated with assets. Health Insurance: Offers coverage for medical expenses, providing financial protection against healthcare costs. Auto Insurance: Protects against financial losses due to accidents or damage to vehicles.

Differences:

- **Mandatory vs. Voluntary Participation:** Social insurance programs are often mandatory for the entire population, with contributions enforced through taxes. Private insurance, on the other hand, is typically voluntary, and individuals choose to purchase coverage based on their needs and preferences.
- **Risk Pooling:** Social insurance relies on the concept of broad risk pooling, where the entire population contributes,

and benefits are distributed based on need. Private insurance involves more selective risk pooling, with policies tailored to individual risk profiles.

- **Redistribution:** Social insurance often involves a degree of income redistribution, aiming to address societal inequalities. Private insurance operates on the principle of risk-based pricing, where individuals with higher risks may pay higher premiums.
- **Government Involvement:** Social insurance is often administered or regulated by the government. In contrast, private insurance is provided by private companies, although government regulations may still apply.

Chapter 28 Life Vs Non-Life Insurance

The distinction between life insurance and non-life (or general) insurance lies in their purpose, coverage, and payout mechanisms.

28.1. Life Insurance:

Objective:

- The primary objective of life insurance is to provide financial protection to the policyholder's beneficiaries in the event of the policyholder's death.

Coverage Duration:

- **Lifetime Coverage**: Life insurance typically provides coverage for the entire lifetime of the insured, although some policies, like term life insurance, may cover a fixed period (e.g., 10, 20, or 30 years).

Beneficiary Payouts:

- **Death Benefit**: The payout in life insurance is the death benefit, which is either a lump sum or periodic payments made to the beneficiaries upon the policyholder's death.

28.2. Types of Life Insurance:

- **Term Life Insurance**: This type of insurance provides coverage for a specified term (e.g., 10, 20, or 30 years). If the insured dies within this period, the beneficiaries receive a death benefit.

- **Whole Life Insurance**: Offers coverage for the entire life of the insured and includes a **cash value** component, which accumulates over time and can be borrowed against or withdrawn.
- **Universal Life Insurance**: A flexible insurance type that combines a death benefit with a savings or investment component, allowing flexibility in both premium payments and the death benefit amount.

Uses of Life Insurance:

- **Estate Planning**: Life insurance can be an essential part of estate planning, ensuring that heirs have financial security.
- **Income Replacement**: It can replace lost income for dependents if the primary earner dies, helping them maintain their standard of living.

28.3. Non-Life Insurance (General Insurance):

Objective:

- Non-life insurance aims to protect against specific financial risks or losses unrelated to the insured's life, such as accidents, property damage, or liability.

Coverage Duration:

- **Limited Duration**: Non-life insurance policies are typically valid for a year or a fixed period, and they are usually renewable.

Beneficiary Payouts:

- **Indemnification for Losses**: Instead of providing a death benefit, non-life insurance policies reimburse or indemnify the insured for losses incurred from specific events, such as a car accident or property damage.

28.4. Types of Non-Life Insurance:

- **Property Insurance**: Covers damages or loss to property such as homes, businesses, and personal belongings.
- **Casualty Insurance**: Provides liability coverage in case the insured is held responsible for bodily injury or property damage caused to others.
- **Health Insurance**: Covers medical expenses, including hospital bills and medication, resulting from illness or injury.
- **Auto Insurance**: Protects against losses due to vehicle-related incidents like accidents, theft, or damage.

Uses of Non-Life Insurance:

- **Risk Mitigation**: Helps individuals and businesses manage the financial risks associated with accidents, natural disasters, or liability claims.
- **Compliance Requirements**: Certain types of non-life insurance, such as auto insurance, are legally required in many regions.

28.5. Key Differences Between Life and Non-Life Insurance:

Aspect	Life Insurance	Non-Life Insurance
Nature of Risk	Covers the risk of the insured's death	Covers various risks such as property damage, liability, and health issues
Payout Mechanism	Pays a death benefit to the beneficiaries	Pays indemnification for specific losses or damages
Policy Duration	Can provide lifetime coverage	Typically has shorter-term policies (renewable)
Investment Component	Some policies include a cash value or investment component (e.g., whole life)	Primarily focuses on risk protection, with no investment component

Life insurance is focused on providing financial protection after the insured's death, while **non-life insurance** covers a broad range of risks unrelated to life and is generally used for short-term risk management.

Chapter 29 Classification of Life, Health, and General Insurance Policies

Insurance policies are broadly classified into three main categories: life insurance, health insurance, and general (or non-life) insurance. Each category serves different purposes and covers distinct risks.

29.1. Life Insurance Policies:

Life insurance provides financial protection to the beneficiaries in case of the policyholder's death. It may also include investment or savings components. The main types of life insurance policies are:

- **Term Life Insurance**:
  - Provides coverage for a specified term, such as 10, 20, or 30 years.
  - Pays out a death benefit if the insured dies during the term.
  - Does **not** include a cash value component.
- **Whole Life Insurance**:
  - Offers lifetime coverage for the insured.
  - Includes a **cash value** component that accumulates over time, combining the death benefit with a savings or investment feature.
- **Universal Life Insurance**:
  - Provides flexibility in premium payments and the death benefit.
  - Policyholders can adjust the coverage amount and premium payments.
- **Variable Life Insurance**:
  - Combines a death benefit with an investment component.

- o Premiums can be allocated among different investment options (stocks, bonds, etc.).
- o Both the **cash value** and **death benefit** may fluctuate based on the performance of these investments.

29.2. Health Insurance Policies:

Health insurance policies are designed to cover medical expenses, providing financial protection against healthcare costs. Common types include:

- **Major Medical Insurance**:
  - o Comprehensive coverage for medical expenses, including hospital stays, surgeries, and preventive care.
  - o Typically includes co-payments, deductibles, and coinsurance.
- **Health Maintenance Organization (HMO)**:
  - o Requires members to choose a primary care physician (PCP) and obtain referrals to see specialists.
  - o Focuses on preventive care and has a network of healthcare providers.
- **Preferred Provider Organization (PPO)**:
  - o Offers more flexibility in choosing healthcare providers, both in-network and out-of-network.
  - o Members generally don't need referrals to see specialists.
- **Exclusive Provider Organization (EPO)**:
  - o Similar to PPO, but usually does not cover out-of-network care except for emergencies.
- **High-Deductible Health Plan (HDHP)**:
  - o Features higher deductibles and lower premiums.
  - o Often paired with a Health Savings Account (HSA) for tax-advantaged savings.

29.3. General (Non-Life) Insurance Policies:

General insurance, also known as non-life or property and casualty insurance, covers a range of risks other than life and health. Common types include:

- **Property Insurance**:
  - Covers damage or loss of physical property such as homes, buildings, and personal belongings.
  - Types include homeowners' insurance, renters' insurance, and commercial property insurance.
- **Casualty Insurance**:
  - Provides liability coverage for bodily injury or property damage caused to others.
  - Includes auto insurance, general liability insurance, and professional liability insurance.
- **Commercial Insurance**:
  - Covers risks related to businesses, including property damage, liability, and business interruption.
  - Types include commercial property insurance, commercial liability insurance, and business owner's policy (BOP).
- **Travel Insurance**:
  - Provides coverage for unexpected events during travel, such as trip cancellations, medical emergencies, or lost baggage.
- **Surety Bonds**:
  - Guarantee that one party will fulfill its obligations to another party.
  - Common in construction projects and other contractual agreements.
- **Marine Insurance**:

- o   Covers risks related to the shipping and transportation of goods by sea or air.
- o   Includes cargo insurance and hull insurance for ships.

Life insurance focuses on providing financial protection for the policyholder's beneficiaries, while **health insurance** covers medical expenses. **General (non-life) insurance** encompasses a broad range of policies designed to cover risks associated with property, liability, and other non-life-related events.

UNIT V INSURANCE DYNAMICS AND REINSURANCE SYSTEM

Chapter 30 Expected Utility and demand for insurance

One important economic model explaining choice of action in uncertain situations is expected utility theory (EUT). The concept of the utility indicates maximization of expected value when making choices; the utility is simply how much satisfactions an individual receives due to an outcome. The concept of EUT has applicability in issues related to insurance because such consumers are insured by their counterparts for some possible damages that might occur.

30.1. Theoretical Framework

People make decision about certain event by calculating the probability for each possible result, and then evaluating its utility in this context, as EUT postulate. Take for example a person who wants to know whether it is necessary to purchase homeowner's insurance cover.

An individual will compare how likely they are to suffer a fire or large loss with how useful any monetary compensation provided in an insurance policy is.

The utility function measures an individual's relative preferences between various ends. However, it is generally presumed, hence people consider smaller gains to be more valuable than comparable losses. It depicts the notion that people are risk adverse and avoid the risks whose benefits have an expected value.

30.2. Insurance Demand and Risk Aversion

Risk-averse people who do not want any unexpected loses will buy insurance to lower it. The individual can ensure that a specific amount is awarded to them during the case of the loss by paying some amount as a premium to the insurer. This creates certainty and thus reduces the overall level of risk.

However, the amount of desired insurance depends on individual's tolerance for risks as well as on how risky it seems to be the insured incident. Risk averse people with high perception of risks will buy more insurance.

30.3. Factors Affecting Insurance Demand

Beyond risk aversion and perceived risk, several other factors can influence insurance demand:

- **Income level:** However, individuals who earn a much income have the capacity to pay for premiums, and relatively less sensitivity in losing a small amount of money.
- **Assets:** Insurance purchase decisions might vary among individuals with different asset endowments whose loss could be absorbed through internal resources.
- **Information availability:** People with greater knowledge on how much loss and the specifics of insurance agreements are more willing to make rational choices on their insurances.
- **Regulatory environment:** Availability and affordability of insurance products are determined by various government regulations that impact the demand for insurance services.

30.4. Alternative Theories of Insurance Demand

Expected Utility Theory has been the major theoretical tool used to explain insurance demand, it however suffers a number of weaknesses like being based on rational choice assumption and not adequately captures the subjective nature of risk perception.

Some alternative views have been put forward; for example, prospect theory suggests that people make decisions based on framing effects as well as losses than on gains (Kahneman & Tversky). Various theories point out that people do not necessarily select actions with highest expected utility, especially about risky and adverse situations.

The concept of expected utility provides a useful basis for analyzing the demand for insurance. Nonetheless, it has its shortcomings and one needs to acknowledge the contribution made by other approaches such as those grounded on psychological reasons and cognitive bias. Finally, it is not a simple issue of buying an insurance because of individual likes, view about risks, and personal economic position.

Chapter 31 Moral Hazard and Insurance Demand

31.1. Key Aspects of Moral Hazard in Insurance:

Moral hazard occurs when individuals or entities change their behavior because they are insulated from the full consequences of their actions, particularly when they have insurance coverage. This can lead to a higher level of risk-taking or less cautious behavior than would occur without insurance.

- **Risk-Taking Behavior**: Individuals or businesses with insurance coverage may feel less responsible for taking precautions. Since insurance will cover the losses, they may be more likely to engage in risky behavior or neglect safety measures.
- **Reduced Incentive for Loss Prevention**: When people know that insurance will cover their losses, they may be less motivated to invest in loss prevention measures, such as security systems or health precautions.
- **Adverse Selection**: Moral hazard can also lead to adverse selection in the insurance market. People who are more prone to risk-taking may be more inclined to purchase insurance, increasing the risk pool for insurers and potentially raising premiums for everyone.
- **Increased Frequency of Claims**: As insured individuals or businesses are less cautious; they may experience more losses. This leads to a higher number of claims, which can impact the cost of premiums and the profitability of the insurer.
- **Insurance Demand**: The willingness of individuals or businesses to purchase insurance depends on various factors, including their perception of risk, the cost of insurance, and

their financial exposure. The demand for insurance rises when individuals feel more vulnerable to financial loss.

31.2. Key Factors Influencing Insurance Demand:

Several factors play a role in influencing the demand for insurance:

- **Risk Aversion**: People who are risk-averse are more likely to seek insurance coverage as a way to mitigate financial uncertainties. Those who perceive higher risks are more inclined to purchase insurance to protect against possible losses.
- **Financial Exposure**: Individuals or businesses with more financial assets or liabilities are more likely to seek insurance. The greater the financial exposure to potential risks, the higher the likelihood they will want to protect themselves with insurance.
- **Regulatory Requirements**: Some insurance types, such as auto insurance or workers' compensation, are legally required. These regulatory requirements increase the demand for these policies as individuals and businesses comply with legal mandates.
- **Perceived Value of Coverage**: The perceived value of insurance is essential in influencing demand. If individuals believe a policy offers significant protection, they are more likely to purchase it. The comprehensiveness of the coverage and the reputation of the insurer can also play a role.
- **Affordability of Premiums**: The cost of insurance premiums is a critical factor. If premiums are perceived as too high relative to the insured party's financial resources, demand for insurance may decrease.

- **Information and Education**: The level of understanding of insurance benefits plays a vital role in demand. Educated consumers are more likely to recognize the importance of insurance in managing financial risks, which can increase demand.
- **Cultural and Social Factors**: Cultural attitudes toward risk and insurance can significantly influence insurance demand. In some cultures, insurance may be seen as essential for financial security, while in others, it may be less emphasized.

31.3. Managing Moral Hazard:

Insurance companies employ several strategies to mitigate moral hazard and control its impact:

- **Deductibles**: A deductible is the amount a policyholder must pay out of pocket before the insurance company covers the remaining costs. By setting higher deductibles, insurance companies encourage policyholders to think carefully before making small claims, as they will bear a larger portion of the cost.
- **Co-Insurance**: Co-insurance requires the policyholder to pay a percentage of the cost of claims after the deductible is met. This helps reduce moral hazard by sharing the financial burden, making policyholders more cautious about unnecessary claims.
- **Risk-Based Pricing**: Insurers use risk-based pricing to set premiums according to an individual's risk profile. Those deemed more likely to file claims due to their behavior or health will face higher premiums. This pricing strategy encourages safer behaviors by linking premiums to the risk level.

- **Utilization Review**: Insurers conduct utilization reviews to monitor the care provided to policyholders, ensuring that only essential services are used. This helps prevent overuse of insurance benefits and ensures cost-effectiveness, reducing unnecessary claims. Additionally, it aids in fraud detection.

Moral hazard in insurance refers to changes in behavior due to the safety net provided by insurance. This can lead to increased risk-taking, reduced investment in loss prevention, and more frequent claims. Several factors influence insurance demand, such as risk aversion, financial exposure, and regulatory requirements. Insurers use strategies like deductibles, co-insurance, risk-based pricing, and utilization reviews to manage moral hazard and control its impact on the system.

Chapter 32 Concept of Risk Management

32.1. Key Elements of Risk Management

Risk management is a structured approach to identifying, assessing, and managing uncertainties and risks that may impact an organization's operations, finances, and reputation. It is essential for good governance and decision-making, ensuring the long-term success and sustainability of the organization.

- **Risk Identification**: The first step in risk management is identifying potential risks that could harm the organization. This involves gathering data from various sources such as marketing, operations, finance, legal, customer feedback, economic factors, industry competitors, and technological advancements.
- **Risk Analysis**: After risks are identified, they must be analysed in terms of their likelihood and potential impact. This analysis helps assess how probable a risk is, its potential severity, and how it could affect the business. This step forms the basis for prioritizing risks based on their seriousness.
- **Risk Evaluation**: Risks are evaluated based on their analysis to determine their severity and how they should be addressed. This step involves ranking the risks according to their potential impact on the organization's goals, financial health, ethical considerations, and regulatory compliance.
- **Risk Treatment**: For each identified risk, appropriate treatment methods are designed. These include various strategies for mitigating or eliminating risks:
  - **Risk Avoidance**: Eliminating the risk by altering plans, policies, or actions to avoid exposure to the risk.

- o **Risk Reduction**: Implementing measures to reduce the severity or likelihood of the risk.
- o **Risk Transfer**: Transferring the risk to a third party, such as through insurance or outsourcing.
- o **Risk Retention**: Accepting the risk, recognizing that some risks are inevitable or manageable.
- **Risk Monitoring**: Risk management is an ongoing process. It involves continuously monitoring risks, reviewing existing mitigation strategies, and identifying new or emerging risks. This helps ensure timely responses to changes and challenges that may arise.

32.2. Importance of Risk Management

Risk management is essential for all organizations, regardless of size or industry, because it:

- **Minimizes Losses**: Identifying and addressing potential risks helps prevent significant losses or damages to the organization's assets and resources.
- **Improves Decision-Making**: Systematic risk assessment enables better decision-making by providing insights into potential risks and their impact.
- **Enhances Operational Efficiency**: By identifying and mitigating risks, organizations can improve their operational processes, reducing disruptions that could hinder performance.
- **Maintains Financial Stability**: Effective risk management helps control unforeseen costs and protects against unexpected financial losses, maintaining a strong financial position.

- **Protects Reputation**: Managing risks effectively helps avoid events that could damage an organization's reputation, ensuring long-term credibility and trust.
- **Ensures Compliance**: Proper risk management identifies and addresses compliance-related risks, ensuring that organizations adhere to legal, regulatory, and ethical standards.

32.3. Risk Management Framework

Organizations often implement standardized frameworks to ensure a consistent approach to risk management. Some widely used frameworks include:

- **Enterprise Risk Management (ERM)**: A comprehensive, organization-wide approach to identifying, assessing, and managing risks across all areas of the business. ERM ensures that risk management strategies align with the organization's overall goals and objectives.
- **Operational Risk Management (ORM)**: Focuses on identifying, analysing, and controlling risks that arise from daily operational activities. ORM helps mitigate risks that can affect the routine functioning of the organization.
- **Information Security Risk Management (ISRM)**: Concerned with protecting the confidentiality, integrity, and availability of information resources. It addresses risks related to data breaches, cyberattacks, and other security threats.
- **Financial Risk Management (FRM)**: Focuses on managing risks related to finances, such as market risk, credit risk, and liquidity risk. FRM aims to minimize the potential for financial losses due to fluctuating market conditions or poor financial decisions.

Risk management is an essential tool for organizations to identify, assess, and address risks that could negatively impact their operations, financial health, or reputation. It is a key element of organizational governance and helps ensure the long-term sustainability of a business. Effective risk management requires continuous monitoring, proper evaluation, and the implementation of strategies to manage potential risks. Frameworks like ERM, ORM, ISRM, and FRM provide structured approaches for managing various types of risks across an organization.

Chapter 33 Elements and Essentials of Risk Management

33.1. Essentials of Risk Management in Insurance

Risk management in insurance involves identifying, assessing, and mitigating risks to protect the organization from potential financial losses. The following are the key elements and strategies essential for managing risks in the insurance industry:

Risk Identification

- **Underwriting Risk**: Evaluating the risks associated with underwriting insurance policies. This involves assessing the risk factors of policyholders, such as demographics, health conditions, lifestyle, and other relevant data to determine the potential for claims.
- **Operational Risk**: Identifying risks related to internal processes, systems, and human factors. This includes errors, fraud, business disruptions, and inefficiencies that could impact the insurer's operations.
- **Market Risk**: Assessing the effects of market fluctuations on investments, including interest rate risk, equity risk, and currency risk that may affect the insurer's investment portfolio.
- **Credit Risk**: Evaluating the risk of default by policyholders, counterparties, or issuers of debt securities held by the insurer. This includes assessing the financial stability of borrowers and counterparty risks.

Risk Assessment

- **Quantitative Analysis**: Using statistical models and data analytics to quantify the likelihood and severity of potential risks. This includes calculations like Value at Risk (VaR) and stress testing to understand the impact of adverse events.

- **Qualitative Analysis**: Assessing the nature of risks and their potential impact on the organization. This involves considering intangible risks such as reputation risk, legal risk, and strategic risk.
- **Scenario Analysis**: Evaluating the effects of various hypothetical scenarios, including extreme or catastrophic events, on the insurer's financial health and stability.

Risk Mitigation and Control

- **Diversification**: Spreading risk across different asset classes, markets, and geographic regions to reduce exposure to any one particular risk.
- **Reinsurance**: Transferring part of the risk to a third party, such as a reinsurer, to limit exposure to catastrophic events and large claims.
- **Risk Retention**: Deciding on the level of risk the insurer is willing to retain, based on its financial strength, risk appetite, and ability to handle potential losses.
- **Operational Controls**: Implementing internal processes, procedures, and controls to reduce operational risks, such as fraud prevention, system security, and workflow efficiency.

Risk Monitoring

- **Key Performance Indicators (KPIs)**: Continuously monitoring KPIs related to risk exposure, financial performance, and other relevant metrics to detect early warning signs of potential risks.

- **Early Warning Systems**: Establishing systems to detect emerging risks or deviations from expected outcomes, enabling timely intervention.
- **Stress Testing**: Running simulations to assess the impact of extreme or unexpected events on the insurer's financial stability and risk exposure.

Risk Governance and Culture

- **Risk Appetite and Tolerance**: Defining the insurer's risk appetite, or the level of risk it is willing to accept, and its tolerance, or the maximum level of risk it can bear without jeopardizing financial health.
- **Board Oversight**: Ensuring active involvement and oversight by the board of directors in the risk management process, providing strategic direction and ensuring alignment with organizational goals.
- **Compliance and Ethics**: Adhering to regulatory requirements and ethical standards to ensure that all risk management practices are aligned with legal and moral obligations.

Communication and Reporting

- **Stakeholder Communication**: Effectively communicating risk management strategies, assessments, and outcomes to key stakeholders such as policyholders, regulators, investors, and employees.
- **Internal Reporting**: Establishing robust internal reporting mechanisms to keep management informed about the status of risk exposures, mitigation actions, and emerging risks.

Adaptability and Innovation

- **Adaptability to Change**: Staying agile and responsive to emerging risks, market dynamics, and evolving business conditions. Adjusting risk management strategies to remain relevant and effective in changing environments.
- **Innovation in Risk Management**: Leveraging technological advancements, such as big data, artificial intelligence (AI), and machine learning, to enhance risk management processes and improve decision-making.

Capital Adequacy

- **Solvency Assessment**: Regularly assessing the insurer's solvency to ensure that it has sufficient capital to cover potential liabilities and unforeseen losses.
- **Capital Allocation**: Strategically allocating capital to different business lines or investments, considering the risk levels associated with each, ensuring sufficient capital reserves for risk coverage.

Insurance Product Design

- **Robust Product Design**: Ensuring insurance products are well-designed to address the specific needs of policyholders while considering potential risks, policy terms, and appropriate pricing strategies.
- **Actuarial Analysis**: Using actuarial methods to assess risk, determine premium rates, and predict the potential future liabilities of an insurance product.

Training and Skill Development

- **Employee Training**: Providing ongoing training to employees on risk management practices, compliance standards, and ethical considerations to ensure they are prepared to identify and mitigate risks effectively.
- **Skill Development**: Building a skilled risk management team with the expertise to assess, analyse, and mitigate risks in a proactive and efficient manner.

Risk management in insurance is critical for ensuring financial stability, protecting against losses, and maintaining operational efficiency. By identifying, assessing, and mitigating risks related to underwriting, operations, investments, and other areas, insurers can safeguard their business and improve decision-making. The framework for risk management includes various elements, such as quantitative and qualitative assessments, diversification, reinsurance, stress testing, and governance. Additionally, embracing new technologies, maintaining capital adequacy, and fostering a culture of continuous improvement are vital for long-term success.

Chapter 34 Risk Assessment

Risk Assessment in Insurance

Risk assessment is a crucial process in the insurance industry, playing a foundational role in underwriting practices and ensuring a company's financial stability. It involves evaluating the potential for losses that could result from insuring an individual or entity, which enables insurers to make informed decisions about offering coverage and setting premiums.

34.1 Functions of Risk Assessment

- **Identifying Risks**: The first step in risk assessment is identifying potential events that could lead to a financial loss for the insurer. These risks can vary significantly depending on the type of insurance being offered, such as:
  - **Natural disasters** (e.g., hurricanes, earthquakes)
  - **Accidents** (e.g., car crashes, property damage)
  - **Health risks** (e.g., illnesses, surgeries)
  - **Death** (e.g., life insurance claims)
  - **Criminal activity** (e.g., theft, fraud)

The risks considered are tailored to the specific insurance product, such as life, health, auto, or property insurance.

- **Assessing Likelihood and Impact**: Once risks are identified, insurers must estimate:
  - **Likelihood**: The probability of each event happening (e.g., the probability of a car accident occurring or a fire damaging a property).
  - **Impact**: The potential financial consequences if the event occurs (e.g., the cost of medical treatments, property repair, or loss of life).

To estimate these factors, insurers often rely on **historical data**, **actuarial tables**, and other relevant statistical tools and models.

- **Risk Scoring and Pricing**: Based on the likelihood and impact of each identified risk, insurers assign a **risk score** to the policyholder or the insured entity. This score reflects the level of risk associated with that individual or asset. The risk score directly impacts the **premium** — the amount the policyholder must pay for coverage. Higher-risk individuals or entities typically face higher premiums because they present a greater likelihood of filing a claim.
- **Risk Mitigation Strategies**: In some cases, insurers may recommend or require **risk mitigation** strategies to reduce the likelihood or impact of certain risks. For example:
  - A homeowner may be asked to install a **security system** to qualify for a lower premium on property insurance.
  - A driver may need to install a **vehicle tracking system** to qualify for reduced car insurance rates.

These strategies not only help minimize potential claims but also encourage safer behavior among policyholders.

34.2 Benefits of Risk Assessment in Insurance

- **Fair and Accurate Pricing**: Risk assessment ensures that premiums are **fair** and accurately reflect the risk posed by each individual or asset. By evaluating the likelihood and impact of risks, insurers avoid **cross-subsidization**, where low-risk policyholders end up paying for the claims of high-risk policyholders. This leads to a pricing structure that aligns more closely with the actual risk associated with a particular policyholder.

- **Informed Underwriting Decisions**: Risk assessment allows insurers to make **informed underwriting decisions**. By thoroughly understanding the risks involved, insurers can decide whether to offer coverage and at what price. This careful evaluation helps insurers maintain their **financial stability** and ensures that they can fulfil their obligations to policyholders by collecting adequate premiums to cover potential claims.
- **Risk Management for Policyholders**: Risk assessment is also beneficial for **policyholders**. By understanding the risks they face, policyholders can take proactive measures to mitigate those risks, which may reduce the frequency or severity of claims. For example, a policyholder might take steps to improve home safety or adopt healthier lifestyle choices. As a result, the policyholder may be able to reduce their insurance premiums, promoting risk awareness and risk reduction.
- **Continuous Monitoring**: The use of technology is increasingly important in risk assessment. Data analytics, machine learning, and **artificial intelligence (AI)** are being used by insurers to enhance their ability to **quantify risks** and make more precise assessments. Additionally, risks are not static and can change over time, so insurers must engage in **ongoing monitoring** and **updating** of risk assessments to ensure they remain accurate and relevant in an evolving risk environment.

Risk assessment is a vital tool in the insurance industry, offering benefits such as **fair pricing, informed underwriting decisions**, and **risk management** for policyholders. By identifying, quantifying, and mitigating risks, insurers can ensure they remain financially sound while offering affordable and effective coverage to policyholders. Technology's growing role, particularly in data analytics and AI, is enhancing the accuracy and efficiency of risk assessment, making it an ongoing process that adapts to new risks and market conditions. Ultimately, this continual evaluation and management of risk contribute to the **sustainability** and **profitability** of the insurance industry.

Chapter 35 Risk Control and Risk Financing

Risk Control and Risk Financing in Insurance

Risk control and risk financing are fundamental components of an insurer's comprehensive risk management strategy. These elements help insurers manage the various risks they face, ensuring financial stability and sustainability in their operations.

35.1. Risk Control in Insurance

- **Underwriting Standards**: Insurers establish **underwriting standards** to evaluate and control the risks associated with the policies they issue. By carefully assessing applicants and setting specific criteria, insurers aim to select risks that align with their **risk appetite**. These standards ensure that the insurer only accepts risks they are prepared to manage, thus controlling exposure to potential losses.
- **Loss Prevention and Mitigation**: Insurers often collaborate with policyholders to implement **risk control measures** aimed at preventing or mitigating potential losses. This may involve:
  - **Guidance on safety practices** (e.g., advising businesses on fire safety protocols or offering training for workplace injury prevention).
  - Offering **discounts** for implementing certain risk management practices (e.g., home security systems or safe driving behaviors).
  - **Risk assessments** to identify vulnerabilities and suggest improvements.

By promoting loss prevention, insurers can reduce the frequency and severity of claims, ultimately benefiting both the insurer and the policyholder.

- **Claims Management**: Efficient **claims management** is crucial for controlling risk. Insurers establish processes to effectively investigate, assess, and manage claims. This ensures that losses are accurately measured and managed, helping to control the overall cost of claims and prevent fraud. A well-organized claims process can reduce administrative costs, improve customer satisfaction, and ensure the financial stability of the insurer.

35.2. Risk Financing in Insurance

- **Premiums and Underwriting**: The **premiums** charged by insurers serve as a primary form of **risk financing**. Premiums are determined based on the risk exposure of the insured and provide the financial resources necessary for the insurer to cover potential losses. Insurers rely on underwriting standards to assess the risk level and set appropriate premiums to ensure they collect enough revenue to cover claims.
- **Reinsurance**: **Reinsurance** is a critical mechanism in risk financing. It involves transferring a portion of the risk to another insurer or reinsurer. This helps spread the risk across multiple entities, reducing the financial burden on any single insurer in the event of large or catastrophic losses. Reinsurance enables insurers to accept more risks and diversify their portfolios, thereby stabilizing their financial operations.
- **Catastrophe Bonds**: Some insurers utilize **catastrophe bonds** as a tool for risk financing. These bonds allow

insurers to transfer specific types of risks, such as those from natural disasters, to the capital markets. Investors in these bonds receive interest payments, but if a pre-defined catastrophic event occurs, the insurer may lose part or all of the principal, which is used to cover the losses. This allows insurers to gain financial protection for rare but severe events.

- **Risk Pools**: **Risk pools** are another form of risk financing in which multiple insurers collaborate to share the risks associated with events. This collective approach helps distribute the financial burden of large losses, making it easier for individual insurers to manage exposure to catastrophic or high-frequency risks.

35.3. Importance of Risk Control

- **Preventing Losses**: The primary importance of **risk control** is to prevent or minimize potential losses. By proactively identifying and addressing risks, insurers and organizations can reduce the likelihood of adverse events occurring, thus protecting their financial health.
- **Enhancing Operational Stability**: Effective risk control measures contribute to the **stability** of operations. By addressing risks, insurers ensure that their activities remain consistent and reliable, even in the face of unexpected challenges or adverse events.
- **Protecting Reputation**: A robust risk control strategy helps protect the **reputation** of the organization. Proactive risk management demonstrates responsibility and reliability, which fosters trust with stakeholders, including customers, regulators, and investors. A company known for good risk control practices is seen as more trustworthy and stable.

35.4. Functions of Risk Control

- **Risk Identification**: The first step in **risk control** is identifying potential risks that may affect the organization. This involves analysing both **internal and external** factors that could impact operations, such as industry trends, economic conditions, and natural disasters.
- **Risk Assessment**: After identifying risks, insurers assess their likelihood and potential impact. This step helps prioritize which risks need immediate attention and which can be monitored. It informs decisions on which risk control measures to implement.
- **Implementation of Controls**: Based on the risk assessment, organizations implement specific measures to control or mitigate risks. These measures may include **preventive controls** (e.g., installing fire alarms or providing safety training) and **mitigative controls** (e.g., offering backup power systems or improving cybersecurity).
- **Monitoring and Review**: Continuous monitoring is essential to ensure that risk controls remain effective. Regular **reviews** and updates are necessary to adapt to changes in the business environment, emerging risks, or changes in regulations.

35.5. Challenges in Risk Control

- **Uncertainty**: Business environments are dynamic, and **uncertainty** is an inherent challenge. Predicting and controlling all potential risks can be difficult due to the unpredictable nature of certain events, such as economic crises or technological disruptions.
- **Resource Constraints**: Allocating resources for comprehensive risk control measures can be challenging,

especially for smaller organizations or those with limited budgets. This can limit the scope of risk management activities, potentially leaving certain risks unaddressed.

- **Resistance to Change**: Implementing new risk control measures often requires changes to existing processes and routines, which may be met with **resistance** from employees or other stakeholders. Overcoming this resistance is essential for the successful implementation of risk controls.

35.6. Importance of Risk Financing

- **Financial Protection**: **Risk financing** provides a financial cushion to protect against unexpected or catastrophic losses. This is crucial for ensuring the organization remains solvent and can continue operations even after significant loss events.
- **Facilitating Business Continuity**: Adequate risk financing ensures that an organization can recover quickly from major losses. It helps maintain **business continuity**, allowing the insurer to continue operations without significant disruptions.
- **Regulatory Compliance**: In some industries, maintaining appropriate risk financing is a **regulatory requirement**. Compliance with these regulations helps organizations avoid legal and financial penalties while ensuring they meet industry standards for financial stability.

35.7. Functions of Risk Financing

- **Premiums and Underwriting**: The premiums charged by insurers allow them to accumulate the necessary financial resources to cover potential losses. Underwriting ensures that policies are issued to acceptable risks, generating sufficient funds for claims.

- **Reinsurance**: By transferring a portion of the risk to a reinsurer, insurers reduce their exposure to large losses. This mechanism enables insurers to share the burden of risk, making their financial operations more sustainable.
- **Catastrophe Bonds**: These bonds provide an alternative form of risk financing, allowing insurers to transfer specific risks to the capital markets. By doing so, insurers can obtain additional financial resources in exchange for the risk of a catastrophic event.

35.8. Challenges in Risk Financing

- **Pricing Challenges**: Determining the appropriate **premium** for insurance policies can be challenging, as it involves forecasting future losses and predicting risk factors that may change over time. Pricing too low may lead to insufficient funds to cover claims, while pricing too high could make insurance unaffordable for policyholders.
- **Market Volatility**: The **reinsurance market** and broader **financial markets** can be volatile, impacting the availability and cost of risk financing options. This market volatility can complicate insurers' ability to secure adequate coverage for large losses.
- **Moral Hazard**: The presence of insurance can lead to **moral hazard**, where insured parties take on greater risks than they would without coverage, assuming that the insurer will cover the losses. This can increase the overall cost of insurance for everyone and lead to higher premiums.

Both **risk control** and **risk financing** are essential to maintaining the financial stability and operational effectiveness of an insurer. Effective risk control helps prevent losses and ensure operational consistency, while robust risk financing mechanisms, such as premiums, reinsurance, and catastrophe bonds, provide a financial buffer against large and unexpected losses. Together, these components form the backbone of a sound risk management strategy that allows insurers to navigate uncertainties while remaining financially viable.

Chapter 36 Worldwide Risk Sharing

Worldwide risk sharing in insurance involves the collective distribution of risk across a network of global insurers, reinsurers, and financial entities. This strategy is essential for managing large, complex risks, particularly those that exceed the capacity of individual insurers. The primary aim is to diversify and share the financial burden associated with catastrophic events or other risks that are too large or complex for a single insurance company to handle independently.

36.1. Overview of Worldwide Risk Sharing in Insurance

Reinsurance:

- **Global Reinsurance Markets**: Reinsurance serves as a critical mechanism for worldwide risk sharing. In this process, reinsurers provide coverage to primary insurers, allowing them to transfer a portion of their risk. Reinsurers may further spread this risk through retrocession arrangements with other reinsurers, creating a global network of risk-sharing.
- **Diversification of Risk**: Reinsurers operate on a global scale, diversifying their portfolios across various regions and lines of business. This diversification helps to stabilize the financial performance of reinsurers by spreading the impact of losses over a wide range of geographic areas and insurance sectors.

International Insurance Programs:

- **Multinational Corporations**: Large multinational corporations often face complex, cross-border risks. To manage these, international insurance programs are designed to provide coordinated coverage across various jurisdictions. This ensures that risks are addressed in a consistent and comprehensive manner across different countries.

- **Specialized Risk Pools**: Certain types of risks, such as those related to terrorism or natural disasters, may require specialized pooling mechanisms. These pools involve a group of insurers coming together to collectively manage and share these specific types of risks across different regions.
- **Global Insurance Policies**: Insurers offer tailored global policies that cover risks in multiple countries. These policies are designed for multinational clients and aim to provide a centralized approach to risk management. By consolidating coverage, these policies simplify administration and ensure more efficient management of multinational risks.

Catastrophe Bonds and Insurance-Linked Securities (ILS):

- **Capital Market Integration**: Catastrophe bonds and other insurance-linked securities (ILS) allow insurers to transfer risks to capital markets. Investors provide funds in exchange for periodic interest payments, and they bear the risk of losing their principal if a specific catastrophic event occurs. This process enables insurers to tap into global capital markets for additional risk financing, thus enhancing their ability to manage large losses.
- **Pooling and Risk Pools**: Global Risk Pools: Certain industries or sectors establish global risk pools, where multiple insurers come together to share specific types of risks. This collaborative approach helps distribute the financial burden of large losses and fosters shared responsibility among multiple parties.

Emerging Technologies:

- **Blockchain and Smart Contracts**: Emerging technologies like blockchain and smart contracts have the potential to improve the efficiency and transparency of worldwide risk-sharing mechanisms. These technologies can streamline administrative processes, making them more efficient, secure, and less prone to error. By facilitating seamless transactions and automating the execution of contracts, blockchain can enable quicker settlement of claims and reduce friction in the risk-sharing process.

36.2. Challenges and Considerations in Worldwide Risk Sharing:

- **Regulatory Compliance**: Operating on a global scale introduces the challenge of complying with diverse regulatory frameworks. Different countries have varying insurance regulations, and managing cross-border compliance can be complicated for both insurers and reinsurers.
- **Currency and Economic Risks**: Fluctuations in currency values and economic conditions can affect the financial stability of global insurers and reinsurers. Economic downturns or inflation in one region can create financial strain for risk-sharing agreements, especially when policies are written in multiple currencies.
- **Legal and Jurisdictional Challenges**: Legal systems and jurisdictions differ from country to country, which can complicate the resolution of claims and disputes. Insurers and reinsurers need to navigate these legal complexities, which may involve international law, local laws, and differing standards for claims settlement.

- **Complexity of Global Risks**: The complexity of managing worldwide risk sharing increases as global risks become more interconnected. Emerging risks such as cyber threats, geopolitical tensions, and pandemics add layers of complexity that require insurers to continually adapt their strategies to effectively manage risks across borders.

Worldwide risk sharing in insurance plays a critical role in managing large and complex risks, especially in a globalized world. Through mechanisms like reinsurance, international insurance programs, and catastrophe bonds, insurers can diversify and distribute the financial burden associated with catastrophic events. However, the practice is not without its challenges, including regulatory compliance, currency risks, legal complexities, and the increasing difficulty of managing emerging global risks.

Chapter 37 Concept and Fundamentals of reinsurance:

Reinsurance is a critical financial arrangement within the insurance industry, where one insurer (the ceding company or primary insurer) transfers a portion of its risk to another insurer (the reinsurer). This process is essential for managing risk exposure, increasing underwriting capacity, and protecting against large or catastrophic losses. By spreading the risk across different parties, reinsurance helps ensure the stability and sustainability of the insurance sector.

37.1. Risk Transfer:

- **Ceding Risk**: The primary insurer cedes a portion of its risk to the reinsurer. This means that the reinsurer agrees to indemnify the primary insurer for certain covered losses. By doing so, the insurer shares the financial burden of claims, which helps spread the impact of losses across a broader base.

37.2. Types of Reinsurance:

- **Treaty Reinsurance**: This is a standing agreement between the primary insurer and the reinsurer to automatically cede and assume risks according to predefined terms. Treaty reinsurance can be:
  - **Proportional Reinsurance**: In this type, the reinsurer agrees to cover a percentage of each policy, meaning that both the premium and the losses are shared proportionally.
  - **Non-Proportional Reinsurance**: This involves the reinsurer covering losses that exceed a certain threshold. The primary insurer retains responsibility for losses up to

the threshold, while the reinsurer covers anything above it.

- **Facultative Reinsurance**: Facultative reinsurance is arranged on a case-by-case basis. The primary insurer decides which specific risks it wants to cede, and the reinsurer evaluates each risk individually before agreeing to assume it.

37.3. Functions of Reinsurance:

- **Risk Sharing and Distribution**: Reinsurance allows the primary insurer to share risks with other insurers, thereby spreading the financial impact of large losses over a broader base. This helps reduce the burden on any single insurer.
- **Capacity Enhancement**: By ceding a portion of the risk to reinsurers, primary insurers can underwrite larger policies or accept more policies than their individual capacity would allow. This helps insurers expand their business and manage a greater volume of risks.
- **Stabilizing Results**: Reinsurance contributes to stabilizing the financial results of an insurer. By mitigating the impact of large, unpredictable losses, it helps smooth out the volatility in an insurer's financial performance.

Reinsurance Premiums:

- **Ceding Commission**: When a primary insurer cedes a portion of its risk, it may receive a ceding commission from the reinsurer. This commission is usually a percentage of the premium ceded and helps offset the costs associated with transferring risk.
- **Reinsurance Premium**: The primary insurer pays a premium to the reinsurer in exchange for assuming a portion

of the risk. This premium is typically calculated as a percentage of the primary insurer's premium income.

Capital Management:

- **Regulatory Requirements**: Reinsurance helps insurers meet regulatory capital requirements by reducing the capital needed to cover potential losses. By transferring a portion of their risk, insurers can lower the amount of capital they need to retain.
- **Financial Stability**: Through reinsurance, insurers can protect their capital and maintain financial stability. This is particularly important when faced with unexpected or significant losses, as it ensures they have the resources to fulfil their obligations to policyholders.

Global Reinsurance Markets:

- **International Collaboration**: Reinsurance is a global industry, and reinsurers operate internationally. This collaboration allows insurers to access a wide range of expertise and capacity from reinsurers around the world, enabling them to manage risks more effectively and share large exposures on a global scale.

Risk Modelling and Analysis:

- **Underwriting and Risk Assessment**: Reinsurers often use advanced risk models and data analysis tools to assess the risks they assume. This helps them set appropriate premiums and manage their own exposure. Sophisticated modelling techniques also enable reinsurers to evaluate the likelihood of catastrophic events and adjust their pricing accordingly.

Challenges and Considerations:

- **Counterparty Risk**: The financial stability of the reinsurer is critical. Primary insurers must carefully assess the creditworthiness and reliability of reinsurers to ensure they will be able to meet their obligations in the event of a claim. Counterparty risk arises if a reinsurer is unable to pay claims when required.
- **Market Conditions**: The availability and cost of reinsurance can fluctuate based on market conditions. Factors like capacity constraints, changes in global risk factors, or the supply-demand balance in the reinsurance market can affect pricing and terms.
- **Complexity**: Managing reinsurance contracts, particularly in a global context, can be complex. Ensuring clarity in the terms, conditions, and coverage provisions is essential to avoid misunderstandings. Effective communication between insurers and reinsurers is vital to ensure that both parties are aligned in their expectations and obligations.

Reinsurance is a key mechanism for risk management in the insurance industry. By transferring risk to reinsurers, primary insurers can protect themselves from large losses, enhance their underwriting capacity, and stabilize their financial results. However, reinsurance involves challenges such as counterparty risk, market fluctuations, and contract complexity, which need to be carefully managed to ensure the effective functioning of the global insurance ecosystem.

Chapter 38 Types of Insurers

Insurance companies, also known as insurers, can be categorized into several types based on the kinds of risks they cover and the range of products they offer. Here's a more refined breakdown of the main types of insurers:

I. Life Insurance Companies

- **Focus**: Specialize in life insurance and related financial products, designed to provide financial protection upon the death of the insured or after a specified period.
- **Key Products**:
  o **Term Life Insurance**: Offers coverage for a specific period (e.g., 10, 20, or 30 years) with a payout only if the insured dies within the term.
  o **Whole Life Insurance**: Provides lifetime coverage, including a cash value component that grows over time.
  o **Universal Life Insurance**: A flexible policy that combines life coverage with an investment savings element. Policyholders can adjust premiums and death benefits.
  o **Variable Life Insurance**: Allows policyholders to invest the policy's cash value in various securities like mutual funds, giving it the potential for higher returns.

II. Property Insurance Companies

- **Focus**: Provide coverage for damage to property and liability for injuries or damages caused to others.
- **Key Products**:
  o **Home Insurance**: Covers damage to homes and liability for accidents or injuries occurring on the property.

- o **Auto Insurance**: Protects vehicles from damages, theft, and accidents. Includes liability coverage for injuries or property damage caused to others.
- o **Commercial Property Insurance**: Protects businesses from damage to physical assets such as buildings, equipment, and inventory.
- o **Liability Insurance**: Offers coverage against legal claims for negligence or harm caused by the policyholder to others.

III.   Health Insurance Companies

- **Focus**: Provide coverage for medical expenses, including hospital visits, doctor consultations, surgeries, and prescriptions.
- **Key Products**:
  - o **Individual Health Plans**: Tailored to individuals or families to cover personal medical costs.
  - o **Group Health Plans**: Often offered by employers, covering employees and sometimes their families.
  - o **Medicare**: A government program providing health coverage for people aged 65 and older or those with disabilities.
  - o **Medicaid**: A government health insurance program for low-income individuals and families.

IV.   Reinsurance Companies

- **Role**: Specialize in providing insurance to primary insurers, helping them manage their risk exposure by taking on some of their risks.
- **Key Function**: Reinsurance allows primary insurers to increase their capacity to underwrite more policies while

maintaining financial stability, especially in the face of large losses or catastrophic events.

V.   Monoline Insurers

- **Specialization**: Focus on offering coverage for a single type of insurance, such as auto, mortgage, or workers' compensation.
- **Niche Expertise**: By concentrating on one specific line of insurance, monoline insurers can develop deep expertise in that area, offering specialized coverage and pricing that larger, multi-line insurers may not.

VI.   Multi-line Insurers

- **Diversity**: Offer a wide range of insurance products across multiple lines, such as life, health, property, and casualty insurance.
- **Advantages**: Multi-line insurers can provide comprehensive coverage for individuals and businesses, often offering bundled policies for convenience and potential cost savings. The diversity in products helps them spread risk and ensure greater financial stability.

The insurance industry is vast and diverse, with companies specializing in life, health, property, reinsurance, and niche areas. Whether offering individual or business protection, insurers are critical to managing financial risk and providing security for individuals and organizations alike.

Chapter 39 Reinsurance Distribution System

The reinsurance distribution system refers to the channels through which reinsurance products are sold and distributed to primary insurers (ceding companies). Reinsurance can be distributed through various methods, and the distribution system plays a crucial role in how reinsurers connect with ceding companies.

39.1. Reinsurance Brokers:

Role: Reinsurance brokers act as intermediaries between primary insurers and reinsurers. They assist ceding companies in finding suitable reinsurance coverage.

Functions:

- Market Access: Brokers have relationships with multiple reinsurers, providing ceding companies with access to a broader market.
- Risk Assessment: Brokers help ceding companies assess their risk exposure and recommend appropriate reinsurance solutions.
- Negotiation: Brokers negotiate terms, conditions, and pricing on behalf of ceding companies.

39.2 Direct Negotiation:

Role: Some large primary insurers, particularly those with significant market presence, negotiate reinsurance directly with reinsurers.

Functions:

- Customization: Direct negotiation allows for more direct customization of reinsurance agreements to meet the specific needs of the primary insurer.
- Cost Efficiency: It may eliminate broker fees, potentially reducing overall costs for the primary insurer.

39.3. Reinsurance Intermediaries:

Role: Reinsurance intermediaries are entities that facilitate the placement of reinsurance by bringing together ceding companies and reinsurers. They may perform certain broker-like functions.

Functions:

- Connecting Parties: Intermediaries connect ceding companies with reinsurers, serving as a facilitator in the placement process.
- Risk Analysis: They may assist in the assessment of risk and structuring reinsurance programs.

39.4. Reinsurance Pools:

Reinsurance pools involve a group of primary insurers that join to share risks collectively. The pool itself may act as a reinsurer to its members.

Functions:

- Shared Risk: Pool members contribute premiums and share the risk collectively, providing a form of mutual reinsurance.
- Pooling Expertise: Pools often have specialized expertise in specific lines of business or types of risks.

39.5. Alternative Risk Transfer (ART) Platforms:

Role: Alternative risk transfer platforms, such as insurance-linked securities (ILS) and catastrophe bonds, offer alternative methods for transferring risk to capital markets.

Functions:

- Diversification: These platforms allow investors to participate directly in assuming insurance or reinsurance risk.
- Innovation: ART platforms provide innovative financial instruments to transfer and securitize risks.

39.6. Technology and Insurtech Platforms:

Role: Technology-driven platforms and Insurtech companies are increasingly playing a role in reinsurance distribution by leveraging digital solutions.

Functions:

- Efficiency: Digital platforms streamline the placement process, making it more efficient.
- Data Analysis: Insurtech platforms may use data analytics and artificial intelligence to enhance risk assessment.

39.7. Global Reinsurance Markets:

Role: Reinsurers often operate in global markets, and ceding companies can access reinsurance capacity from around the world.

Functions:

- Diversity: Ceding companies can choose from a diverse range of reinsurers with different specialties and risk appetites.
- Capacity: Access to global markets increases the capacity available for reinsurance.

39.8. Considerations and Challenges:

- Regulatory Compliance: Reinsurance distribution must comply with various regulatory requirements, which can vary by jurisdiction.
- Data Security: The increasing use of technology in reinsurance distribution raises concerns about data security and privacy.
- Market Dynamics: The reinsurance market is influenced by factors such as supply and demand, pricing trends, and the overall economic environment.

Chapter 40 Reinsurance Markets in India

The reinsurance market in India has undergone significant evolution, driven by regulatory reforms and an increasing presence of both domestic and international reinsurers. The **Insurance Regulatory and Development Authority of India (IRDAI)** plays a pivotal role in overseeing and regulating the reinsurance landscape, ensuring market stability, and fostering growth.

In recent years, India has witnessed a gradual opening of its reinsurance sector to global players, which has led to enhanced competition and better risk management solutions. Domestic reinsurers, such as **General Insurance Corporation of India (GIC Re)**, continue to hold a significant share of the market while international reinsurers have increasingly expanded their operations, strengthening the capacity and innovation within the sector.

Regulatory developments, such as the **IRDAI's Reinsurance Regulations**, have aimed at streamlining operations, improving transparency, and ensuring adequate risk retention for insurers. These regulations also emphasize the importance of maintaining solvency margins, prudent underwriting practices, and comprehensive reinsurance arrangements to manage systemic risk in the Indian market.

The reinsurance market's growth is further fuelled by India's expanding economy, rising insurance penetration, and an increasing number of large-scale infrastructure projects that require complex and diversified coverage. Reinsurance companies are now more actively involved in handling catastrophic risks, with a growing demand for specialized products such as **catastrophe bonds** and **insurance-linked securities (ILS)**.

40.1. Opening of the Reinsurance Sector:

India has gradually opened its reinsurance market to foreign reinsurers. Prior to these changes, the General Insurance Corporation of India (GIC Re) held a monopoly on reinsurance in the country.

- **Regulatory Framework:** The IRDAI regulates the reinsurance sector in India, and it periodically reviews and updates the regulatory framework to enhance market competitiveness and efficiency.
- **International Players:** With the liberalization of the reinsurance market, several global reinsurers have set up branch offices or entered into partnerships with Indian insurers. This has increased the diversity of reinsurance options available to Indian insurance companies.
- **GIC Re:** GIC Re (General Insurance Corporation of India) is a government-owned reinsurance company and has played a historically dominant role in the Indian reinsurance market. It continues to be a significant player even as competition has increased.
- **Reinsurance Brokers:** Reinsurance brokers play a crucial role in facilitating transactions between primary insurers and reinsurers. They assist in placing risks with both domestic and international reinsurers.
- **Alternative Risk Transfer:** There is a growing interest in alternative risk transfer mechanisms, including insurance-linked securities (ILS) and catastrophe bonds. These instruments provide additional options for managing risks.
- **Technology Integration:** Insurtech and technology-driven solutions are gradually becoming part of the reinsurance landscape in India. These innovations aim to improve

efficiency, enhance risk assessment, and streamline processes.

- **Catastrophe Risk Management:** Given the country's vulnerability to natural catastrophes, catastrophe risk management and reinsurance solutions are of particular importance in the Indian market.

40.2. Challenges and Considerations:

- **Risk Perception and Modeling:** Accurate risk modeling, especially for natural catastrophes, is crucial. Developing a comprehensive understanding of risks is essential for both reinsurers and primary insurers.

- **Market Penetration:** Despite growth, insurance penetration in India is still relatively low. This affects the size and potential of the reinsurance market.

- **Regulatory Compliance:** Compliance with evolving regulatory requirements and standards poses challenges, especially for new entrants in the market.

- **Capacity Building:** Building the capacity to underwrite and manage diverse risks, including emerging risks, is an ongoing consideration for reinsurers operating in India.

- **Global Economic Factors:** Global economic conditions and geopolitical factors can influence the reinsurance market in India, affecting pricing, capacity, and overall market dynamics.

Bibliography:

- Insurance Regulatory and Development Authority of India (IRDAI). (2023). *Reinsurance Regulations and Guidelines.* Retrieved from https://www.irdai.gov.in
- General Insurance Corporation of India (GIC Re). (2023). *Annual Report.* Retrieved from https://www.gicre.in
- Swiss Re Institute. (2022). *World Insurance Report.* Swiss Re, Zurich.
- KPMG India. (2021). *India Reinsurance Market: Current Trends and Future Prospects.* Retrieved from https://home.kpmg/in
- S&P Global Market Intelligence. (2021). *India's Insurance and Reinsurance Market: Opportunities and Challenges.* Retrieved from https://www.spglobal.com
- IRDAI (Insurance Regulatory and Development Authority of India). (2020). *Annual Report: The State of the Indian Insurance Sector.* Retrieved from https://www.irdai.gov.in

References:

- Insurance Regulatory and Development Authority of India (IRDAI). (2023). *Reinsurance regulations and guidelines.* Retrieved from https://www.irdai.gov.in
- General Insurance Corporation of India (GIC Re). (2023). *Annual report.* Retrieved from https://www.gicre.in
- Swiss Re Institute. (2022). *World insurance report.* Swiss Re, Zurich.
- KPMG India. (2021). *India reinsurance market: Current trends and prospects.* Retrieved from https://home.kpmg/in
- S&P Global Market Intelligence. (2021). *India's insurance and reinsurance market: Opportunities and challenges.* Retrieved from https://www.spglobal.com

- IRDAI (Insurance Regulatory and Development Authority of India). (2020). *Annual report: The state of the Indian insurance sector*. Retrieved from https://www.irdai.gov.in